WHAT PEOPLE ARE SAYING ABOUT

Broken Heart on Hold

We have been married for forty-seven years and have been involved in marriage ministry for over thirty of those years. During that time we have been privileged to gain much insight into marriage, both through our own experience and in sharing with others. We know that the recovery process involved in renewing a troubled marriage often follows a painful and tortuous path, requiring dedication and commitment from both spouses. Linda Rooks has done a brilliant job of describing and detailing the process of recovery from the brink of marital disaster. Linda effectively chronicles the pain experienced by both spouses and shows that the presence of God on the journey provides the hope necessary to persevere. While we are not speaking on behalf of any ministry, we personally believe that the book would be a valuable resource for all couples, no matter what their current situation happens to be.

—PAT AND ROGER BATE
FORMER INTERNATIONAL COORDINATORS, RETROUVAILLE INTERNATIONAL

Stunning vulnerability! Linda Rooks may be the most courageous author I have ever read. She takes deep, vague, painful feelings and puts them into words with which you can identify—and find relief. Every gripping story will give you wisdom, encouragement, hope, and a map through the shadowy world of broken marriage. If it were up to me, there would be a law that no man could ever leave his wife without first reading this remarkable book.

—PATRICK MORLEY
AUTHOR; FOUNDER AND CEO, MAN IN THE MIRROR

Linda Rooks has written captivating stories of stark reality, yet they are embedded with God's healing and hope. This book is for people who discover the home they thought they had is now gone and they are wandering in the wilderness toward an unseen promised land. Filled with practical insights and written with almost poetic devotion, you will gain strength and help in time of need. Broken Heart on Hold *is essential reading for those who are wondering if they should give up. The answer is … well, read the book.*

—DR. JOEL C. HUNTER
SENIOR PASTOR, NORTHLAND—A CHURCH DISTRIBUTED,
ORLANDO, FLORIDA

As an expert on marriages in crisis, I highly recommend this book! Linda Rooks brings hope and healing to the brokenhearted. She comes alongside readers and walks them, step-by-step, through the dark valley and toward The Light.

—NANCY C. ANDERSON
MARRIAGE EXPERT AND AWARD-WINNING AUTHOR OF *AVOIDING THE GREENER GRASS SYNDROME: HOW TO GROW AFFAIR PROOF HEDGES AROUND YOUR MARRIAGE*

Broken Heart on Hold *is an excellent resource for women experiencing the complex and heart-wrenching trauma of separation. With biblical inspiration, Linda Rooks offers strength and nuggets of hope to those caught in marital limbo. This resource reveals how God brings purpose to our pain.*

—LAURA PETHERBRIDGE
SPEAKER, AUTHOR OF *WHEN YOUR MARRIAGE DIES—ANSWERS TO QUESTIONS ABOUT SEPARATION AND DIVORCE*

Women going through a painful divorce or separation are sure to feel a hug of encouragement as they read Broken Heart on Hold! *Linda truly understands the emotional roller coaster of a gut-wrenching separation and shares practical insights and biblical wisdom that will give hope to weary hearts even if reconciliation doesn't occur. The easy-to-read format also makes a great daily devotional.*

—LEANN WEISS
PRESIDENT OF ENCOURAGEMENT COMPANY AND BEST-SELLING *HUGS*™ AUTHOR

Linda Rooks has found the answers to help unravel the most complex problems that impact couples facing divorce. These strategies will work to save marriages, and somebody you know needs this book today!

—DWIGHT BAIN
NATIONALLY CERTIFIED COUNSELOR, CERTIFIED FAMILY LAW MEDIATOR, AND AUTHOR OF *DESTINATION SUCCESS*

For the person who is hurting from a broken marriage (or one who is counseling) this book offers solution and hope. Linda Rooks has been there and gives daily practical steps toward a healing heart and possible reconciliation in a marriage.

—VONETTE Z. BRIGHT
CO-FOUNDER, CAMPUS CRUSADE FOR CHRIST, INTERNATIONAL

Broken Heart on Hold

SURVIVING SEPARATION

LIFE JOURNEY®

Bringing Home the Message for Life

COOK COMMUNICATIONS MINISTRIES
Colorado Springs, Colorado • Paris, Ontario
KINGSWAY COMMUNICATIONS LTD
Eastbourne, England

Life Journey® is an imprint of
Cook Communications Ministries, Colorado Springs, CO 80918
Cook Communications, Paris, Ontario
Kingsway Communications, Eastbourne, England

BROKEN HEART ON HOLD

The Web site addresses and books recommended throughout this book are offered as resources to you. These resources are not intended in any way to be or imply an endorsement on the part of Cook Communications Ministries, nor do we vouch for their content.

Cover Design: Greg Jackson, Thinkpen Design, llc
Cover Photo Credit: ©Creatas Images

First Printing, 2006
Printed in the United States of America

1 2 3 4 5 6 7 8 9 10 Printing/Year 11 10 09 08 07 06

All Scripture quotations, unless otherwise noted, are taken from the *Holy Bible, New International Version®. NIV®.* Copyright © 1973, 1978, 1984 by International Bible Society. Used by permission of Zondervan. All rights reserved. Scripture quotations marked HCSB are taken from the *Holman Christian Standard Bible®,* Copyright © 1999, 2000, 2002, 2003 by Holman Bible Publishers. Used by permission; quotations marked NASB are taken from the *New American Standard Bible,* Copyright © 1960, 1995 by The Lockman Foundation. Used by permission; quotations marked TLB are taken from *The Living Bible,* © 1971, Tyndale House Publishers, Wheaton, IL 60189. Used by permission; quotations marked RSV are taken from the Revised Standard Version Bible, copyright 1952 [second edition 1971], Division of Christian Education of the National Council of the Churches of Christ in the United States of America. Used by permission; quotations marked NRSV are taken from the New Revised Standard Version Bible, copyright 1989, Division of Christian Education of the National Council of the Churches of Christ in the United States of America. Used by permission. All rights reserved; quotations marked NLT are taken from the *Holy Bible, New Living Translation,* copyright © 1996. Used by permission of Tyndale House Publishers, Inc., Wheaton, Illinois 60189. All rights reserved; and quotations marked KJV are taken from the King James Version of the Bible. (Public Domain.)

ISBN-13: 978-0-7814-4439-2
ISBN-10: 0-7814-4439-X

LCCN: 2005939113

I thank my God every time I remember you.
—PHILIPPIANS 1:3

To three faithful friends who walked beside me through my darkest hours and were always there for me with hope and encouragement:

Toni Jo Kidd, a frequent companion who took many long walks with me through my crisis, giving me a shoulder to lean on, encouraging my heart, listening to my fears, uplifting my spirit, and helping me laugh;

Kathy Herrbach, whose friendship became a special port in the storm by challenging me with God's perspective, helping me keep focused, and letting me pour out my heart;

Mary Johnston, my long-time friend, who traveled with me through spiritual valleys and tunnels to help me find precious nuggets of truth.

You are the women who modeled a special friendship to me, a friendship I now hope to share with women walking through the pages of this book.

CONTENTS

Acknowledgments 11
Introduction: Let's Take a Walk 13

PART 1
HOLDING TOGETHER A BREAKING HEART

Beyond Broken Dreams 16
When It Doesn't Make Sense 18
Ripped Apart 19
The Beginning of Our Madness 21
Facing a Four-Legged Stool 25
Roller-Coaster Emotions 27
Friends for the Journey 28
Spiritual Muscles 30
Take Care of Your Body 31
Fear 33
When Anger Turns Red 34
Out of Control 36
A Coffee Break with God 38
The Back Burner 40
Amanda's Story 41

PART 2
A SAFE PLACE FOR YOUR HEART

A Safe Place for Your Heart 48
Unconditional Love 49
Withdrawal 52
Where Do I Begin? 54
Letting Go 56
Time Can Be Your Friend 58
The Years of the Locusts 60
Seeing the End from the Beginning .61
Chicken Soup 63
Keeping Your Focus 64
The Beach Ball 66
The Puzzle 67
All Things New 70
Before All the World 72

PART 3
SEARCHING YOUR HEART

Migrating South 80
Going Deeper 82
Seeing with New Eyes 84
Weeds 86
Detours 88
Looking for the Light 90
No Place to Go 93
Healing Lips 94
A Journey of Suffering 96
A Spiritual Sacrifice 98
Living Stones 100
Silver and Gold 102

Water into Wine 105
Without a Road Map 107

PART 4
HEART CONNECTIONS:
WALKING THROUGH THE SHARDS

If No One Sees 114
Sweet Dependence 115
Hanging On 116
Weapons 118
How Much to Say to Whom 120
Discouraging Words and Encouraging People 122
Children Caught in the Pain 125
Temptation 127
His Strength in Our Weakness 130
If 132
The Unseen Battle 133
A Practical Guide to Spiritual Warfare 135
Burned Potatoes 138
A Healing Salve 140
Shadows 142
When Beautiful Things Die 143
A Change of Direction 145
The Quietness of Your Heart 148
From Love and Back Again 149

PART 5
A RESTORED HEART

The Journey 156
Against the Undertow 157
Standing Firm 159

Extinguishing the Arrows 162
Great Mysteries 164
Love's Paradox 167
The Power of Praise 169
Walking on the Water 172
Epilogue 174

Readers' Guide 177
Recommended Resources 187
Topical Index 190

ACKNOWLEDGMENTS

$\mathcal{M}$y special thanks to the following people who helped bring this book into being:

My husband, Marv, for the 100 percent support he has given me throughout the process of working on this project and for his continued enthusiasm in sharing the hope we found together;

Author Pat Morley and his wife, Patsy, for their early encouragement and support;

Pat Verbal, who was the first person to suggest that *Broken Heart on Hold* would be a worthwhile project to pursue;

My editor, Mary McNeil, for believing in me and turning *Broken Heart on Hold* from a dream into a reality;

Dr. Joel Hunter, senior pastor of Northland, A Church Distributed, for his insight and words of wisdom that have encouraged me over the years, some of which have made their way onto the following pages;

Becky Hunter, for her continued support and encouragement;

Pastor Carl Stephens, for his forthright teaching and exhortation and for permitting me to borrow some of his insights for the benefit of my readers;

Julie Wolf, LMHC, for her professional counseling perspectives in reviewing this book;

Roger Shepherd, LMHC, for being a wonderful, supportive, and wise counselor;

Debra Tomaselli, who shared her talent and skills in critiquing my manuscript;

The many people who allowed me to share their stories so others could find hope;

And most of all, my precious Lord who gave me the promise of Romans 8:28: "In all things God works for the good of those who love him, who have been called according to his purpose."

You stand in the middle of a time warp. Past and
present events swirl about with incomprehensible
speed and craziness. But for you, personally, time is
standing still. You are paralyzed.

This book is a love gift to you, the woman whose
marriage hangs in the balance and who doesn't know
what to do. This book of encouragement was written
to be a friend who can walk beside you in this
desperate time of loneliness—to uplift, challenge, and
support you, all the while offering hope and pointing
you to God.

LET'S TAKE A WALK

*N*ot long ago I was in a place where I suspect you may
be right now. My heart was broken. It was as if I were
wandering through a dark tunnel and couldn't see the way
out. For three long years, my husband and I were separated.
For two years before that the tension in our home had kept
me continually off balance. I struggled to make sense of
what was happening in my life. Eventually the winding
roads brought me to the end of that dark tunnel—and I
found that the sun was actually shining. Our marriage was
healed; we reconciled in 1998.

Now I want to walk through some of those valleys with
you. I know how lonely it is. Let me be your friend. Together we
will search the corners of possibilities, cry when the shadows
seem to overtake us, and celebrate when we find answers.

Broken Heart on Hold is meant to be a friend to walk
beside you through the labyrinths of your confusion and
pain. It is not a quick fix or a prescription for how to solve
your problems. It is intended to be a daily companion in
your crisis. It is not a book to be picked up and read through
once and then set on the shelf. Rather, I suggest you read
one selection each day and let the devotional thoughts sink
into your heart and mind. Mull it over. Chew it up. Then the
following day go on to the next.

But that suggested pattern is not a formula or system.
You may want to just keep reading. That's okay. I know you
are hurting, and you must choose your own pace and
rhythm. But if you do read ahead and take it in all at once,
go back later, start at the beginning, and reread one selection

each day. When we pour water over hard, crusty ground, it runs off and little is absorbed into the firmly packed earth. It takes time to sink in. Similarly, when we are hurting and our spirits are dry, we must give words of healing time to soak in and soften up the soil of our souls. Reading each entry one at a time—either initially or later—will gradually bring you to a place of peace and strength.

When a particular issue crops up and you need help immediately, use the topical index at the back of the book to find a selection that fits your needs. A resource section provides recommendations for books and programs that offer more in-depth help for your particular situation.

In each of the other sections are true stories of women who struggled with marriage crises and made it through, not only with their marriages intact, but with better marriages. And throughout the book you will meet many women (and some men) who wrestled with different marital issues and arrived at a variety of results. Their struggles are transparent and their stories are true, but to maintain privacy, names have been changed and identities slightly obscured.

Because focusing is often difficult in the middle of crisis, I invite you to visit my Web site at www.brokenheartonhold.com where I have individually formatted a number of Bible verses for your strength and encouragement. From my Web site you can download full-color pages of whatever Scripture you choose and post it on your wall, mirror, or refrigerator so you can see it regularly and be encouraged. When our minds are spinning in different directions, being reminded of a Scripture can lead us to a more peaceful and healthy path.

There is hope at the end of the tunnel, and I believe that you can find it. I'd like to accompany you on this journey. Let's set out to find the light.

A Note to Men: Although *Broken Heart on Hold* is addressed mainly to women, if you are in marital crisis you are welcome to join us. Feel free to look over my shoulder as I talk with the woman walking beside me. Men as well as women have already found comfort and hope in the material on the following pages.

Part 1

HOLDING TOGETHER
A BREAKING HEART

*He heals the brokenhearted
and binds up their wounds.*
—Psalm 147:3

BEYOND BROKEN DREAMS

I will make rivers flow on barren heights, and
springs within the valleys. I will turn the desert into
pools of water, and the parched ground into springs.

—ISAIAH 41:18

*A*s I awake from a brief, unsettled sleep, the tension gripping my body draws me back to the shadowy stillness of the bedroom and the sense that something is wrong. What is the nightmare still clinging to my mind? I close my eyes again, the dark dread growing inside me. Even without looking, I feel the empty space in the bed stretching out beside me in the dark.

This isn't a dream. This nightmare is real.

I fight back the encroaching fear threatening to overtake me. Then the floodgates open and memories rush in. He's left me. I am alone. *How could he do this to me? How could he actually leave me?*

But he has, Linda. He has left you. The memory of a friend's words from the day before pierce my heart. My body trembles. I feel myself sinking into a dark hole. *He has left you.* Inside my head the tension grows like a balloon filling too rapidly, stretching to the breaking point. I cry out—terrible sobs breaking from the deep caverns of my soul.

That's how the day would often begin for me. Chances are you've been there. Perhaps you're there now, maybe not because your husband physically walked out the door, but because, in one way or another, he has left you emotionally. It could be another woman, an irrational anger that has closed the doors of his heart, or an eternity of nights when the silence between you gnaws relentlessly at your insides. You know the pain I'm talking about, and you're looking for a way out. You're looking for hope.

In the middle of this dark valley, one fact is absolutely clear: The pain that has entered your life is real. It is inescapable and will not go away. But what do you do with it?

If we bury our pain, it will only resurface somewhere else. If we slam the door on it, we will open another door along the way and find ourselves face-to-face with it again. Pain can change form, but it doesn't disappear.

But there's another transformation our pain can make. On my journey down this difficult path, I discovered that the one who created the majesty of the universe and brought life from the dust of the earth, the one who dissolved the power of death into the miracle of eternal life, the one who healed the lepers and paralytics, also promised to heal the broken-hearted and bind up their wounds.

He is talking about us. We are the brokenhearted. And the powerful God of the universe wants to heal our wounds.

Hope squeezes through the taut sinews of our fear and leads to life when we place our pain in the hand of the Creator. In his hands the brokenness of our hearts becomes fresh, warm clay that he molds into something beautiful and new. Only our Creator has the power to transform our pain into hope.

But you must linger with him. Keep your eyes upon his face, his words within your heart. Let his love hold you above the shards of broken dreams. Run to him now. Surrender to God the broken pieces of your heart. Let him hold you in the shelter of his arms. Let him carry you through the barren valley and along the road to springs of living water where hope resides.

Find rest, O my soul, in God alone;
my hope comes from him.

—PSALM 62:5

When It Doesn't Make Sense

Look upon my suffering and deliver me,
for I have not forgotten your law.
Defend my cause and redeem me; preserve
my life according to your promise.

—Psalm 119:153–154

*W*hen the person who promised to love and cherish you for the rest of your life walks out the door or abandons you emotionally, it doesn't make sense. You committed yourselves to one another for a lifetime. You thought your spouse regarded that commitment the same way you did. Now that commitment appears to have been an illusion. Something entirely different is going on in your mate's mind, and your marriage hangs in the balance.

Your mind races out of control. How did this happen? *What happened?* When did it start? What is he going to do? *What will I do?* Your body feels as though it is tearing apart. And, in fact, your life *is* being ripped apart. If you ever get to sleep at night, you wake in the morning thinking it has all been a nightmare. But chances are you've hardly slept. And it's not a nightmare, it's real.

When our perception of the world collides with reality, and we can no longer process it mentally, physically, or emotionally, that is when we need to process it spiritually. Only on a spiritual level can it make sense. Only when we go deeper into the spiritual realm by spending more time with God and his Word and seeking the wisdom of other Christians can we get beneath the pain that comes from something that doesn't make sense.

You may well have just entered the most intense spiritual experience of your life. Choose this day to look up to God rather than down into the abyss of your circumstances. You may never again experience anything so intensely painful, but God is standing there beside you. Reach out to him. Let him hold you.

*Do not be far from me, for trouble is
near and there is no one to help.*
—PSALM 22:11

RIPPED APART

*I loathe my very life; therefore I will give
free rein to my complaint and
speak out in the bitterness of my soul.*
—JOB 10:1

*P*acing back and forth in front of the upstairs window
and then down the hall and back again, I busied myself
by picking up an out-of-place object in one room and taking it
to another. Every couple of minutes I returned to the bedroom
and glanced through the frame of navy blue curtains, watching
each car that came around the corner.

My husband had told a mutual friend of ours that he would
finally come over and talk to me. That was four days ago, and
I'd still not heard from him directly. The hurt and anger trembling within me began to bubble up, boiling to the top.

"Why doesn't he come over or at least call me?" I yelled at
the empty room. "It's been four weeks since he left, and he
won't even talk to me. Why is he doing this? What have I done
to him? I'm like a piece of garbage he left in a dump. Why does
he hate me?"

My anguish erupted in anger from my lips and a flood of
tears from my eyes as I threw myself onto the bed. I could not
stand the awful pain. Death could not hurt worse than the pain
that was ripping me apart.

In those early days of our separation, I walked around in a daze, going through the motions of living. My mind was a jumble. Nothing made sense. When the raw, jagged emotions cut through my exterior and I flailed about hysterically, my daughters stared at me, not knowing what to say or do. Seeing their shock and helplessness, I realized it was unfair to push my pain onto them. After all, they were hurting too. I could not go on this way. I had to find something to hold on to. I had to find someone to help steady me. Finally, when my tears were exhausted and my anger was spent, I cried out in despair to God.

When someone wrongs us and inflicts enormous suffering on us, anger and resentment are natural reactions. We feel trapped in giant emotions, and the broken foundations of our thinking and decision making lie in pieces at our feet. We feel imprisoned by the chaos and irrationality of our circumstances. *This should not be happening. I trusted him, and he should not be doing this!*

At certain moments, a healthy awareness of our own legitimate claim to fairness is unleashed, and we lash out in anger. Anger is normal, even necessary right now, and bottling it up can be unhealthy. Anger, as well as depression and denial, is a natural part of the grief process and should not make us feel guilty. In fact, Ephesians 4:26 says, "Be angry but do not sin" (RSV).

Expressing your anger in appropriate ways is important to help you become healthy and functional again. Writing your feelings in a journal and talking to friends and counselors are healthy outlets. Exercising can release some of the pent-up feelings that hold you captive. Even expressing your anger to your husband under the right conditions is essential for your ultimate healing.

But for the present, there is no simple antidote for this agony and no simple resolution to this crisis. Only in the deeper mysteries of God can healing begin and hope be found. For with God, a broken heart is not the end result but a transition. Your pain can become an open door for God to enter in and touch you in the deep places of your life—if you will let him.

Just for a moment, stop and listen for God's voice. He calls through the gaping wounds of your heart. "Be still," he says, "and know that I am God" (Ps. 46:10). Let his voice woo you to his side. In the stillness he can enter into the acute suffering that has taken control of your life and bring his light into your darkness. He knows about suffering. He knows the overwhelming sorrow of rejection. He walked this earth in the form of a man and shared in our miseries, even to the point of death. He's been there in the lonely crowds of accusers, humiliated by the very people he came to love. Let him be your refuge and strength, your comforter and advocate, the one who heals you. Let your affliction become an open door that lets him into your life so he can touch you and bring a mystery of blessing from your deep hurt.

> God, let me feel your touch upon my life. Hold me in your arms. Show me the light that can illumine my darkness. Heal my broken heart.

THE BEGINNING OF OUR MADNESS

*T*he scent of the roses teased at my mind in cruel confusion as I stared at the flower arrangement sitting by the front door. *Why did he send me flowers?*

My husband had left me four weeks earlier without explanation and told a mutual friend that he planned to stay away for an indefinite period of time. "He says he couldn't go on with it the way it was," this friend had told me. "You don't have anything in common anymore, and he needs to find out who he is. He's content now, just chilling out, reading a new book each day."

My heart felt like it was splitting in two. My mind was spinning. *Separated for an indefinite period of time?* What did that mean? Months? Years? Why wouldn't he talk to me? I would listen to him—hear what he had to say—if he would just talk to me. Instead of telling me his intentions, he was ignoring me.

And now Mother's Day flowers with a card signed "Love." The ends of the knot tightening inside my head constricted a little more. What did *this* mean? What was he doing to me? Was this a prelude to his coming over to talk? Or was this a way to circumvent a conversation with me?

That night in bed I pulled the covers over my chest and stared at the phone on the nightstand. *Should I call and thank him?* No. It was up to him to call me. *But he won't call.* The flowers were a means of avoidance. *He won't call.* Pain seared my soul as I cried.

The next day I drove to the condo where he was staying to thank him in person. Perhaps he'd talk to me then—explain his intentions, tell me what he was thinking.

When he came to the door, I was nervous but tried to sound upbeat.

"I wanted to thank you for the beautiful flowers," I said.

"Thanks. I'm glad you liked them." He smiled uncomfortably. He appeared agitated, distant. "I can't talk now." He stepped back and shut the door.

I stood in front of the closed door, stunned. Heart pounding, I got in my car and steered toward home. When I entered the house, I fell trembling onto the sofa, hot tears filling my eyes, anger curdling in my veins. Early in our marriage we had called each other halves; we had been so in love. And now it felt as if half of me was literally tearing away from my body.

Spying his picture on the cabinet, my thoughts wandered back to when we first married. I was standing on Point Loma wearing his favorite red dress, excitement and euphoria fogging my mind as I watched my husband's ship come around the bend of the land. We'd been married only a month before he went to sea for a nine-month tour of duty with the navy.

Through binoculars I picked out my tall, lanky lieutenant on the bridge of the ship, his shoulders slightly stooped in his characteristic stance. My heart skipped a beat. When the ship drew beside the pier and they lowered the stairs, I barely got to the top before he grabbed me in his arms, knocking my hair askew. I sank into the warm curve of his body. We often described the San Diego apartment we lived in during those navy days as "our blue heaven."

In a cloud of memories I rose from the sofa and went to the garage in search of the letters he had written me while he was deployed. I plopped a stack beside me and began to read. *I love you so deeply, Darling, and hope you think of me every second of the day as I do you. Your picture is about worn-out as I pull it out of my wallet so much.* My heart constricted into a ball of pain. We had been so much in love. What happened to us?

I thought about how angry he'd been at a family barbecue the summer before. It was so unlike him. I didn't understand where it was coming from. We'd had the typical problems—financial mostly—but nothing unusual, and as a family we'd had lots of fun together over the years. Our daughters—one now in college, the other a teenager still at home—had both added tremendous joy to our lives.

I remembered another outburst a few years earlier. My husband had risen in anger from the kitchen table and spouted off a litany of my commitments. "Everything's more important than me. I'm the last thing on your list of priorities."

Our mutual friend had said my husband was seeing a counselor and was open to me seeing her too. I called for an appointment.

"I was reluctant at first to see you, since your husband is my client," the counselor said as we met in her office days later. "But I called him and he said it was all right."

"I just want to know what's going on," I said, feeling the veins on my neck standing out. "I don't understand what he's doing."

"Do you love him?" she asked.

"Yes." I tried to keep my voice under control. "We've had problems, but I never doubted that he loved me. I never thought he'd leave me." Every nerve ending prickled inside my body. "That's one thing I never thought he'd do." My voice broke into a high pitch as a sob caught in my throat.

The counselor arranged a meeting between my husband and me at her office. We sat on opposite sides of the room—my husband appearing confident and comfortable in the controlled setting, while I was frightened to hear what he was about to say. We had been apart six weeks.

"I was surprised you took this so hard," he said. "I didn't think you'd care that I left. I thought you'd be relieved."

"You didn't think I cared?"

"We've been living two separate lives."

"I do care. I love you," I said.

"How do you feel about that?" the counselor asked him.

"Well—good."

"Would you like to work on the marriage?" she asked him.

He looked at me, then looked away. "I don't know if Linda can accept me for who I am now."

That summer we began dating and fumbled through a number of counseling appointments. In the fall he moved back home. But our reconciliation lasted only two months before the vermin that had been eating away at our relationship raised its ugly head once more. He left again, this time talking divorce. The problems ran much deeper than we had yet addressed. The layers piled on top of one another in a mountain of misunderstandings and bad decisions. Nine months of our nightmare had passed, and the end was not yet in sight. More than two excruciating years still remained. It was a time of confusion and turmoil.

In those bleak hours it was hard to imagine that life with the very same person could ever get better. But God had begun to get my attention. And he had much to show me.

FACING A FOUR-LEGGED STOOL

Why are you downcast, O my soul?
Why so disturbed within me?
Put your hope in God, for I will yet praise
him, my Savior and my God.

—PSALM 42:11

*W*hen confusion descends upon you so quickly, it is as though you are suddenly trapped in a giant cobweb, and no matter how you try it is impossible to untangle the strands. How can you break free of this terrible web of confusion?

During the turbulent years of my separation, my pastor, Joel Hunter, encouraged me to remember when I was a young child and the circus would come to town. Brightly colored posters were displayed on walls and billboards advertising the coming event. One of the images was the fierce-looking lion growling at the lion tamer. In one of the lion tamer's hands was a whip, in the other a four-legged stool. As my pastor pointed out, it was easy to understand why the tamer held the whip. But why the stool? What did a four-legged stool have to do with taming a lion?

Joel explained that when a lion tamer holds a stool up to a lion with the legs pointing forward, the lion tries to focus on all four legs at once and becomes confused. This positioning is what gives the lion tamer control.

Sometimes, in a crisis such as this, we become like the lion: trying to focus on all that is happening around us, our minds blur. We attempt to analyze all the events and details leading up to our crisis, yet still can't grasp their meaning. We contemplate the possible solutions and outcomes, but find few answers and more questions. When our whirling minds steer us in new directions, our feelings change from day to day. One day all the facts line up one way, and on the very next, all the facts line up another. Alarmed by our turbulent emotions, we strive to understand our own contradictory behavior. We are like the lion trying to focus on all four legs of the stool at the same time. The result is total confusion.

The only way to get beyond this confusing state is to locate the lion tamer behind the stool and concentrate on him. In our situation God is the lion tamer. He is in charge of our circumstances. If we focus clearly and consistently on him, our focus will be clear, peace will replace confusion, and our actions can take a rational course.

However, even while we are focusing on the lion tamer, the legs of the stool may continue to distract us. When that happens, confusion will follow, and the constant turmoil makes it extremely hard for us to keep our focus continually on God. We need help.

One helpful tool to stay focused during difficult times is to keep a journal. Expressing thoughts and emotions on paper crystallizes them. After expressing my confusion in writing, I was able to put those particular musings to rest and walk away from them for a period of time. Keeping a journal also provides continuity to help us get a clearer grasp of the true situation. Contradictions in thoughts and emotions from day to day or from week to week are revealed, and you can see where you've been, where you are, and, perhaps, where you're going.

The Lord is near. Do not be anxious about
anything, but in everything, by prayer
and petition, with thanksgiving, present
your requests to God. And the peace of God,
which transcends all understanding, will guard
your hearts and your minds in Christ Jesus.
—PHILIPPIANS 4:5–7

ROLLER-COASTER EMOTIONS

Show me your ways, O LORD, teach me
your paths; guide me in your truth
and teach me, for you are God my Savior,
and my hope is in you all day long.

—PSALM 25:4–5

Your mind is swirling. Your emotions spiral upward in anger only to crash into the bottomless pit of depression a few minutes later. You feel as though you are on an emotional roller coaster taking you from the intense pain of sadness to an energized state of anger, then into a leveling-off period where you are crying out to God. And as you feel each emotion, you're certain it is a permanent state.

While your mind swirls, let God capture your thoughts and draw them inward to examine your own life. Search the Scriptures. Allow God's Word to speak to you.

John Gray's book *What You Feel You Can Heal* (Heart, 1994) has some insightful revelations that may help you get hold of your feelings so you can unravel and heal them. One of his principles is that anytime you feel *stuck* in a particular emotion, such as anger, you are actually experiencing four other emotions at a subconscious level. To become *unstuck*, Gray contends that you must successfully work your way through all five emotions.

To do this, he suggests writing a love letter to your spouse, expressing your feelings and your reasons for each: anger or blame; hurt or sadness; fear or insecurity; guilt or regret; then ending with your feelings of love and forgiveness, which he believes lie beneath the others. Writing one of these letters (which you do not intend to send), may help you unravel your deep feelings to bring about some stability in your emotional state.

Whatever tools you use to help get through this time, remember that your emotions will not subside immediately. Give this painful time to God, and let him use it to reveal things within you that will ultimately bring about a new and better life in the future, whether it is with or without your husband.

God, steady my emotions. Give me your peace. Show me your truth.

Friends for the Journey

If one falls down, his friend can help him up.
But pity the man who falls and has
no one to help him up!

—Ecclesiastes 4:10

The hour was late as I stood at Toni Jo's front door and rang the bell. The porch light flicked on, and I saw her face peek around the door. Her expression told me she knew something was wrong even before I opened my mouth.

"I got on I-4 with thoughts of either heading toward Canada or driving into Lake Ivanhoe, but I decided to come here instead," I said, allowing the absurdity of my words to communicate the heaviness of my heart.

Her eyes met mine, gently probing my thoughts. "Didn't go well, huh?" she said, knowing that my husband and I had a "meeting" that evening.

"Could you take a walk?" I asked.

We wound our way beside the lake shimmering beneath a

fractured moon, then continued up and down the quiet streets of her neighborhood. She listened as I struggled through my painful story, then she asked questions to help me search my heart. She encouraged me with hopeful observations and even made me laugh. Toni Jo was a friend who walked beside me both physically and emotionally.

On a Sunday morning I sat at the back of the church and waited for another friend—Kathy—as she finished putting communion dishes away. We took a drive together, and I shared the confusion of my broken heart. I needed advice. She listened with gentle understanding, asked insightful questions, and challenged me with God's perspective. Kathy and I had lunch together often. She saw to it that not too much time elapsed between get-togethers. Her gentle wisdom often shed a glimmer of light on my dark path.

Mary and I had been friends for a long time. Because of the depth of her relationship to God, she was able to walk my emotional and spiritual labyrinths with me, looking for nuggets of gold.

These three friends—and others—were love gifts from God. They gave me strength when mine was gone and watched with me for the light to shine through. When at last it did, they celebrated with me.

You may or may not have friends right now that you can count on. If you do, you are blessed and should let them minister to you. If you don't, seek someone out. To bridge the gap for you in these times of emotional distress, it is important to find Christian friends, a pastor, or a counselor you can trust to listen and keep your confidence. You need friends who will listen without being judgmental, who understand that your intense heartache will result in reactions that may not be typical of you.

Don't be afraid to ask for help. Not having friends to share the load can exact a heavy toll.

Begin to identify women you can connect with, who will listen and encourage, who won't try to create shortcuts and suggest you give up. Counselors can be helpful, too. Don't be ashamed to ask for recommendations at your church. A Christian counselor may be invaluable for providing the bread crumbs that lead you down the path toward home. This journey may take awhile, and you need patient, caring companions along the way.

> *There is a friend who sticks closer than a brother.*
> —Proverbs 18:24

Spiritual Muscles

> *Being strengthened with all power according to his glorious might so that you may have great endurance and patience, and joyfully giving thanks to the Father, who has qualified you to share in the inheritance of the saints in the kingdom of light.*
> —Colossians 1:11–12

Have you ever exercised so intensely that when you finally stopped, you couldn't move for a while because your muscles felt so weak? I felt this way after a ten-mile walkathon and again after working out on a new machine at the gym. The muscles in the stressed part of my body felt almost paralyzed. Of course, I was soon able to move them again, and furthermore, I found that if I kept using those muscles, they became stronger.

Spiritual muscles work the same way. When a crisis first hits us, it is almost impossible to stay focused on the Lord. We try to pray, read the Bible, look to God. But our minds swim around in memories, imaginations, and a myriad of fears. Our only petition to God is the one enormous question that continually echoes in our heads: WHY?

We may be too emotionally weak to get out of bed, too weak to pick up the phone and call a friend, too weak to set our minds on God. The spiritual muscles that keep us focused on God instead of circumstances may feel extremely out of shape. But just like getting back on that exercise bike builds up our physical muscles, continuing to go back to God strengthens our spiritual muscles. Practical helps such as listening to Christian music and teachings, talking to Christian friends, and singing praises can pull us out of our confused emotions and provide the strength to refocus our thoughts and prayers.

If you want to rejoice at the "shape" your life is in when you've made it through this time, you need to exercise and strengthen those spiritual muscles.

I will strengthen you and help you; I will uphold
you with my righteous right hand.

—ISAIAH 41:10

TAKE CARE OF YOUR BODY

Do you not know that your body is a temple
of the Holy Spirit, who is in you, whom
you have received from God? You are
not your own; you were bought at a price.
Therefore honor God with your body.

—1 CORINTHIANS 6:19–20

Are you eating these days?" Toni Jo asked. "Looking at you, I think it's a good idea we decided to meet for lunch today." Her eyes twinkled mischievously, but I knew her question was serious. I had lost a considerable amount of weight.

Taking a seat opposite her at the table, I sighed. "I just don't have any appetite anymore."

"I wish that was my problem." She laughed. "I want to eat everything in sight."

We women often pride ourselves on our ability to keep our emotions under control for the sake of others. Throughout most of life we keep a pleasant countenance and continue on with our duties regardless of how we feel. You may not have encountered a life experience like this, one in which your emotions grabbed control and dragged you through valleys as frightening and lonely as the one in which you find yourself today. During this agonizing time, you truly have achieved enormous success if you finish the day in one piece and with your basic responsibilities accomplished. But in the turmoil, what may go overlooked is you. In the struggle just to keep up, you may yield to the temptation to ignore your own body. You may not have any appetite or you may overeat to soothe the hurts and grief that overwhelm you. You may not sleep as you wrestle through the night with memories, fears, and imaginations. Or you may not be able to get out of bed in the morning.

You are precious to God. He does not want you to suffer physically from the neglect you may unconsciously inflict on your body. Take whatever steps are necessary to keep from damaging your health. Try to eat healthy foods and exercise every day. Limit your intake of caffeine, sugar, and alcohol. If you can't sleep, or if you sense that your emotions are leading to dangerous physical manifestations such as heart palpitations or shortness of breath, see a doctor. If depression continues too long, you may want to tell your doctor about that, too. Medications may help during this critical period. This troubled time will end, and when it does, you will want to have a healthy body.

Be merciful to me, LORD, for I am faint;
O LORD, heal me, for my bones are in agony.

—Psalm 6:2

FEAR

You are [Sarah's] daughters if you do what is
right and do not give way to fear.

—1 PETER 3:6

ear is probably one of the most pervasive emotions when we are separated from our spouses. Security has evaporated and our world is upside down. We have every reason in the world to feel overcome with fear.

But fear can be a driving force that not only binds us up emotionally but also causes us to take unfortunate and hasty actions.

Because we may feel so caught off guard by what has happened, we are like sentries protecting the walls of our lives to make sure nothing will harm us again. We may take deliberate measures to protect ourselves from future deceptions and attacks, and we are suspicious of everything our mates do.

While we should be wise and proceed with caution, prayerfully asking God for direction in our particular situation, we also need to conscientiously continue to "do what is right and … not give way to fear." A deliberate, cautious, and prayerful attitude is appropriate as we move forward from day to day. We must not allow fear to dictate our actions.

"But," you ask, "with my life so out of control, how do I keep fear from overtaking me and dictating my behavior?" The verse preceding the verse above gives the answer. It says the holy women of the past "put their hope in God" (1 Peter 3:5).

We can try all the worldly tactics we want, but it is likely the world that has pervaded our relationship to allow the catastrophe that came upon us. God holds the key. Our hope rests in him. He alone can show us the way. God is the one who holds all things together (Col. 1:17). Keep your eyes on Jesus. Let him be your focus. Let him guide you step by step. Do not waver.

The LORD is my light and my salvation—
whom shall I fear?
The LORD is the stronghold of my life—
of whom shall I be afraid?

—PSALM 27:1

Blessed is he … whose hope is in the LORD
his God, the Maker of heaven and earth,
the sea, and everything in them—the LORD,
who remains faithful forever.

—PSALM 146:5–6

WHEN ANGER TURNS RED

For the mind set on the flesh is death, but the
mind set on the Spirit is life and peace.

—ROMANS 8:6 NASB

The muscles in her neck tensed, and her face flushed in anger as she described what had taken place. Her husband had left and was treating her in an emotionally abusive manner. Her life was torn apart, her children were suffering, and her soul was tormented. Her wounded spirit cried out for revenge against the man who had betrayed his promise to love her for a lifetime. As she continued telling me her story, however, I saw that her anger had turned into bitterness, and that the bitterness was causing more damage to her and her children than it was to her husband.

It was good she was talking to me. She could vent her painful feelings and let me move through them with her to a more peaceful place. She needed a friend who could understand, put an arm around her, and let her talk. I understood. I'd been there too.

At times like this, when our minds whirl through the happenings of the past weeks or months, collecting bitter memories that eat us up inside, we cry out for the justice and respect we deserve. We are angry, and the pain inside demands that we express it. Anger is not wrong, but the Bible counsels us to "Be angry but do not sin" (Eph. 4:26 RSV). The admonishment within that liberating counsel is that we must use care to express our anger in healthy ways.

If we allow our anger to take control, it can become a cancer that destroys us inside while spreading out and killing our relationships. It can cause havoc in our families and add further destruction to our children, our spouses, and ourselves if we say and do things we later regret. God said he will be our avenger. As much as we want justice, we may be limited in what we can and should do right now. In fact, letting our minds dwell on thoughts of retribution is what the Bible alludes to as the mind set on the flesh, and the Bible says that "the mind set on the flesh is *death*."

But the mind set on the spirit is *life and peace*. While the anger inside needs to be released in healthy ways, it can be redirected by calling on the name of Jesus and letting him take control. Setting our minds on the Spirit will fill us with his peace.

Consciously and forcefully turn your eyes upward to Jesus rather than inward toward your turbulent feelings or outward toward the one who hurt you. Allow God to show you the spiritual dimensions of what is happening to you. Your anger may very well be justified. But what you are ultimately angry with is the fallen nature of your husband, whatever form his fallenness has taken.

From Adam and Eve to Abraham and Jacob, all the way to David and Solomon, and on to Peter and Paul, we see in Scripture that we are all part of the fallen nature. None of us is exempt. Some sins are more obvious and hurtful than others, but sin is common to us all. This doesn't excuse anyone who falls into sin, but recognizing our common sin nature may enable us to borrow a little of God's bountiful grace to soften the intensity of our anger.

Make a sign that reads "Part of the Fallen Nature," and put it in your car, on your refrigerator, or wherever you will see it often. Whenever feelings of betrayal and bitterness arise, let that sign be a reminder that what you have witnessed in your husband is part of the fallen nature that is common to us all.

Then continue to immerse your mind and emotions in God. Set your mind on the Spirit, and you will know his peace and experience his life welling up within you. As long as your eyes are on him alone, your anger will not control you.

My eyes are ever on the LORD, for only
he will release my feet from the snare.
Turn to me and be gracious to me, for I am
lonely and afflicted. The troubles of my heart
have multiplied; free me from my anguish.
—PSALM 25:15–17

OUT OF CONTROL

The peace of God, which transcends all
understanding, will guard your
hearts and your minds in Christ Jesus.
—PHILIPPIANS 4:7

How do we keep our emotions from running away with us?

When life turns upside down, emotions become so strong and overpowering that they seem to have a life of their own. They race out of control, and we can do little to restrain them. But emotions seldom occur in a vacuum. They result from our thoughts.

Under normal circumstances we recognize the connection between mind and emotion. We watch a scary movie and we experience fear. We think about a compliment someone paid us and it brings a smile of pleasure. We think of how someone wronged us and we feel angry.

But now you sometimes wake with fear gripping your heart. You open a drawer and find an old anniversary card from your husband and then burst into tears. You run into an acquaintance who innocently says to say hello to your husband and panic grips your heart. You don't *ask* for these feelings or choose these thoughts. They just happen.

Expect these sudden "collisions of heart" to periodically send you reeling into painful flashbacks. But during the normal course of the day, you can lessen emotional turmoil by policing your thoughts.

What we think about—whether true or imagined—affects our emotional state. If you think about your profound hurt, then deep depression, anger, or confusion will undoubtedly follow. Remembered actions or words of betrayal stab us with enormous pain. If we speculate about the future, tremendous fear rises up. Sometimes it is difficult to discern what is true and what is only conjecture and imagination.

Because of the confusion of this time, it is absolutely vital that you push your way through to what is absolutely true. And that absolute truth is that God loves you, and he is in control. As confusing as everything is right now, your circumstances are only temporary. You can only count on them being true for today or yesterday, but tomorrow is in God's hands—and tomorrow can change.

God is the ultimate truth. He is the same yesterday, today, and tomorrow. He has not changed and will not change. Take hold of him. Feast your eyes and heart and mind on God, the ultimate truth. Meditate on him and his Word.

You won't find it easy to keep focused on God. You will be tempted to divert your gaze to the right where your anger is close at hand, or to the left where depression waits. But talk to God and ask him to help you stay focused on him. Set your mind on the Spirit, not on the flesh. Actively seek him, and he will sustain you.

To help you focus on the Lord, here are a few tips:

- Listen to a praise CD.
- Sing favorite hymns or praise songs.
- Go to www.brokenheartonhold.com and download one or more Scriptures. Then tape them up where you will see them often.
- Read your Bible until your mind rests on words of healing.
- Call a Christian friend.
- Surround yourself with the things of God.

A COFFEE BREAK WITH GOD

*Let the beloved of the LORD rest secure in him,
for he shields him all day long, and the
one the LORD loves rests between his shoulders.*
—DEUTERONOMY 33:12

*L*ook at it as a time to rest, to get your house in order, and to spend some quality time with the kids," my hairdresser advised me when I came in looking physically worn-out and emotionally distraught. She had heard from mutual friends that my husband had left, but she hadn't planned to say anything. My hairdresser was a cheerful woman who never interfered in other people's problems, but she had gone through some of her own in the past.

"I used to look at those times as a chance to get a break from all the fighting and stress that had been going on in the home," she said. "Take this as an opportunity to do the things you couldn't do otherwise. Don't let him get the best of you with his little temper tantrum."

Her voice rose with an unusual amount of passion. "That's what it is: He's a little boy throwing a temper tantrum. Don't let yourself get sentimental about things. Think about your kids and what's best for them. And think about what God wants you to do."

However you may feel about my hairdresser's assessment, the practical advice has a lot of merit. If you are currently separated, look at this as a rest time with God, a little coffee break in your life when you and God can sort out some of the strains and uncertainties that have taken place in your marriage. It can be a healthy approach.

Have a gift exchange with God. Give your worries and fears to him, and in exchange he will give you his peace and rest. Then, in your period of rest, have the confidence that God is working out the details according to his best plan. Meanwhile, take the opportunity to do something you've been putting off. Clean out closets. Organize the garage. Go on special outings with the kids. Take the time to listen to them—find out what they're thinking and feeling about things. Have that garage sale you've been putting off all year. Look at it as a rest from the friction in the home.

If you continually wander back to *the worries,* put some praise music on while you work. It will help keep the eyes of your mind on Jesus while you keep your hands busy with productive work.

Whatever happens, these projects are things you can be glad you did. If he comes home and things between you are good, you'll have cleaner closets and happier kids. If he doesn't come home, at least you'll still have cleaner closets and happier kids—one of the more profound spiritual truths in this book.

We wait in hope for the LORD;
he is our help and our shield.
—PSALM 33:20

THE BACK BURNER

*The Lord is near. Do not be anxious about any-
thing, but in everything, by prayer and petition,
with thanksgiving, present your requests to God.*

—PHILIPPIANS 4:5–6

Y ou need to stop thinking about him and concentrate on
yourself," my friend told me over coffee one afternoon.
"Put him on the back burner. Make *yourself* your priority, and
listen to God."

It was nine months since my hairdresser had said something similar. And here I was again. My husband and I had been
through two months of counseling, and he had moved back
home for a couple of months. Now he was gone again. We were
back where we started, and things seemed more hopeless than
ever. When my friend suggested putting my husband on the
back burner, I was ready to go deeper.

This became a time for God to be personal with me as he
showed me how he could take care of me and ways he wanted
me to grow. I could do nothing about my husband, but God
was in control of this out-of-control situation and had purposes
of his own that he wanted to accomplish. My job was to find
out what he was doing and go along with it.

I went to church services more often and tuned in to
Christian radio. I hung out at libraries and bookstores, reading
personal enrichment books. I startled my children by listening
seriously to their criticism and allowing myself to consider
whether some of it was true. I asked trusted friends for honest
input. Most important, I tried to pay attention to the quiet
nudges of God as I pored over the Scriptures and sought him
through prayer.

A few years after God enabled my husband and me to put
our marriage back together, I talked with a friend who was in

the process of a divorce. She told me she had held herself accountable to three mature Christians who similarly counseled her to take the time to work on herself before making decisions. At first she balked at their suggestion, but a year later was glad that she had followed their advice. Although her path and mine led to different destinations, at the end of both our difficult journeys we agreed that we were better, stronger women, closer to God, and able to see good coming out of our ordeal.

Chances are good that you need to hear this advice too. Instead of trying to make major decisions at this point, step outside the whirl of emotions and unreliable thought patterns and listen for God's voice. Remember the image of the lion and the four-legged stool? Set your mind on the Holy Spirit, not on the flesh. Let God's Spirit strengthen you and build you up so you are able to make good decisions from a prayerful and careful attitude. Moving forward from a spirit of prayer rather than reacting to mere circumstances will set in motion things that you are proud of later.

Wait for the LORD; be strong and
take heart and wait for the LORD.
—PSALM 27:14

AMANDA'S STORY

They stood in her living room, holding each other, sobbing. "You don't have to do this," she said to him. "You can still change your mind." She could tell by the look in his eyes that he still loved her. Why was he doing this? "Pete," she said again, "you can still change your mind."

But he didn't.

The next day they sat across the table from each other in the judge's chambers. Amanda tried to catch Pete's eye, but he avoided her look.

How had they come to this point?

Several years earlier, Pete had stood on a scaffold at the house he had built for them in the woods overlooking the river. In one hand he held a hammer. A pouch full of nails was fastened to his belt. The breeze ruffled his black hair. Stopping momentarily to gaze out over the water, a look of wistfulness and excitement lit up his eyes.

He had poured a lot of love into that house. Amanda could see that now. He'd built it himself. Designed it too.

Amanda cringed as she thought about what happened next. They had never been good with money, but after they built the house, the credit cards seemed to take on a life of their own. She bought new furniture, accumulating huge debts. The incomes they brought in were no match for what they owed. They missed mortgage payments. Finally, the bank foreclosed on the house.

She winced at her insensitivity at the time. "We'll just have to start over," she had said to Pete as she helped load the living room sofa onto the truck. "It'll be okay."

But it wasn't okay. Pete was devastated. His dream was lost. Soon he began talking about divorce. But to Amanda it was just words. He wasn't serious. He was just upset.

She eventually came to understand, however, that he was all too serious. She came face-to-face with that realization during a session at her counselor's office.

"What is your worst fear?" the counselor had asked.

"Divorce." A picture had risen in her mind at the time. She and Pete were standing on the seashore. Waves were crashing. Like a child, she clung to him, wrapping herself around him with both arms and legs.

After they separated, several single women from church saw their opportunity with Pete and went after him. Amanda felt sick. She accepted a better paying job in California and urged Pete to go with her. Although he drove the truck to move her and the children out west, he returned home once his family was settled. Four months later, on Christmas Day, he surprised the family by showing up at the door. Amanda thought things were finally turning around. But Pete had a hard time finding a job. When he was offered a well-paying, short-term job in Antarctica, he took it. Once out of the country, he seldom called.

Amanda gradually realized that Pete was trying to get as far away from her as possible.

Each night she lay in bed wondering what was going on, hot tears wetting her cheeks. In anguish she cried out to the Lord. "God, I know somewhere in your Word you said you would be a husband to the widows. I know I'm not a widow, but, God, I'm without a husband. Jesus, hold me. I hurt so much. Please, Jesus, hold me." A peace enveloped her as she felt the presence of the Lord enfolding her in his arms.

One night God renewed the picture she'd had in the counselor's office. Again she and Pete were standing on the seashore. But this time she and Pete stood next to each other. The waves still threatened, but she was standing up. After that she knew she would be okay. She was beginning to get stronger.

By a fluke of circumstances, Amanda discovered she had symptoms of ADHD, which she learned was a major factor in her money-management troubles. She began taking medication and jubilantly told Pete she'd found the answer to their problems. He wasn't convinced.

When Pete returned from Antarctica, he rented an apartment nearby. Every Tuesday and Thursday he had dinner with Amanda and the children. And every week Amanda was sure that things would get better. Each time he jumped on his motorcycle and left for his own apartment, her heart sank all over again.

She opened her Bible to the Psalms, reading one passage after another, the words running through her mind like water on dry land. "Hang on," the Lord seemed to say to her. In the stillness of her heart, that was all she heard.

Meanwhile, Pete filed for divorce.

Amanda continued to cry out to God. "God, why are you letting this happen? I know you hate divorce. I'm praying according to your will. I know I am. So why, God? Why isn't anything happening to turn this around?"

She could no longer focus on God. She could no longer cope. She needed some answers. What other changes could she make?

She poured out her heart to her counselor. His reply struck her as odd. "You need to grieve the loss of your marriage," he said. "You need to sit in your grief."

"Sit in my grief?" she asked. "I don't have any idea how to do that."

Her mind was in a muddle as she left his office. *Sit in my grief?* She got in her car and turned on the ignition. As she thought about the counselor's words, she remembered the story of Job and his friends sitting with him in his grief. She turned out of the parking lot and headed home.

"God, come and sit with me in my grief," she prayed. "I don't know how to do it. Show me how to grieve." Suddenly, the emotions that had been wrenching her apart bubbled to the surface. She couldn't choke back her tears. They were like a gusher bringing up all the hurt and pain. She grasped the steering wheel, her chest heaving in and out, cleansing tears washing down her cheeks while she tried to navigate through the streets.

When she pulled into the driveway, she was exhausted. But it was a turning point. Suddenly she saw that the breakup of her marriage wasn't all her fault. Pete was responsible too. She saw with a new perspective, with more clarity. She'd tried so hard to restore her marriage, but it was time to release it. She had to let go.

By the time the divorce was finalized, Amanda was stronger, even though her heart was broken. She was more confident and was learning to deal with her medical condition.

When Amanda discovered that Pete was continuing to see a woman from the church back home, it was a painful blow, but she could see that she did not want her old marriage back. If they were ever to reunite, it would have to be a brand-new relationship.

Amanda and Pete stayed connected and continued doing things as a family. With no expectations from each other, Amanda felt a new freedom to be herself. She no longer tried to impress Pete. When she decided to buy a motorcycle, Pete helped her pick it out, then helped her learn to ride it. There was a new openness between them. They were becoming two whole people.

Several months later, Pete began to search his heart. He broke off the relationship with his girlfriend.

One crisp February morning, Amanda and Pete went out to breakfast. Afterward, they drove to her home, pulled into the driveway, and sat in the car talking. Pete turned to Amanda and took her hand, then quietly waited until she looked into his eyes.

"You can ask me anything about anything, and I will tell you the truth," he said.

Amanda's heart began to pound. After all the waiting, all the tears, and all the hope that never had materialized, this day had finally come. As they discussed the hurts that had built over the preceding years, she saw his humility, his transparency, and she knew his heart had changed. In their nineteen years of marriage, he'd never been this open.

"I think I've been living out the greener-grass syndrome," he told her. "Only there isn't any greener grass. I've been spending the last four years looking for a better Amanda, but there isn't one."

They remarried a few months later, and their new marriage became a thousand times better than they ever imagined. Their experience apart deepened their appreciation for one another. Instead of taking each other for granted, they put each other's needs on an equal plane with their own by practicing mutual biblical submission. They learned the futility and danger of getting upset over minor irritations. With more self-confidence, Amanda began giving Pete the affirmation he needed, and they built a friendship they never had before.

Foundational to it all was Amanda's learning not to look to a person to meet all her needs for security. That is God's job. And God proved to her that he is very faithful in carrying it out.

Part 2

A SAFE PLACE FOR YOUR HEART

A broken and contrite heart, O God, you will not despise.

—PSALM 51:17

A SAFE PLACE FOR YOUR HEART

Above all else, guard your heart,
for it is the wellspring of life.

—PROVERBS 4:23

Y ou stand in a desolate valley. In the distance, peaks of lush mountain ranges thrust upward, shrouded in patches of cloud. But between you and the mountains a vast wasteland unfolds. The parched earth stretches for miles on every side, scorched by the blazing sun.

Kicking the crusty dirt at your feet, you watch a dry dust cloud rise and disperse in the air. A light film settles on your hand, which is tightly clenched before you. Slowly, you open your fingers and look with alarm at the splintered, disfigured pieces of your broken heart within your grip. Your husband's face appears before you, hovering like a shadow, familiar but unfamiliar with eyes that will no longer meet your own.

A gentle touch on your arm compels you to look up. Jesus stands before you. Against the bleakness of the valley behind him, his garments shimmer like white gossamer. The light radiating from his face encompasses you in a circle of radiance. His eyes immediately draw you, and they penetrate you deeply with gentle warmth, an unfathomable, deep-rooted, overflowing love.

Jesus holds out his hand to you, palm open, the wound left by the cruel nail still visible. You read the words of invitation in his eyes. He asks you to give him the fragments of your heart, to place them on the nail print in the palm of his open hand. You look down at the broken pieces wrapped tightly in your fist.

Jesus' outstretched hand waits patiently.

At this moment Jesus invites you to put your heart with all its brokenness in the shelter of his waiting hand. His love reaches out through time to woo you. It calls to you through the beauty of creation, the mournful wailing of the prophets, the blood trickling from the crown of thorns, and the hope of new life radiating from the empty tomb. His hands, though mighty and strong enough to calm the storm, are tender as they reach out to comfort and heal.

Trust God now to hold your heart in the protection of his loving care. Do not bury it in the hard ground or give it back to your husband. Trust it to the one who binds up the broken-hearted. He knows how to put together all the pieces so your heart will be safe and strong, yet soft, supple, and warm.

Then, as you begin to heal, pray that your husband, too, will eventually place his unsteady heart into God's care. Only when both of your hearts are in the safety of God's loving protection will love be free to flow between your husband's heart and yours once more.

> *The peace of God, which transcends all*
> *understanding, will guard your*
> *hearts and your minds in Christ Jesus.*
> —PHILIPPIANS 4:7

UNCONDITIONAL LOVE

> *And I pray that you, being rooted and estab-*
> *lished in love, may have power, together with all*
> *the saints, to grasp how wide and long and high*
> *and deep is the love of Christ, and to know this*
> *love that surpasses knowledge—that you may be*
> *filled to the measure of all the fullness of God.*
> —EPHESIANS 3:17–19

*T*wisting my wedding rings back and forth on my finger with my thumb, I stopped to look at them, the light dancing brilliantly over the many facets of the diamond. I'd worn them for so long that they were almost like a part of my hand. My mind traveled back to that moment in time—a fairy tale away—when my husband slipped the wedding ring on my finger, a symbol of our eternal love.

My heart grew sick and heavy. *Eternal love? Till death do us part?* Where were those promises now? How I had wanted a love that would last forever and bind us together through a lifetime. But it was just a myth. Love didn't last forever. At least it didn't for me.

As women, we ache for a love that will hold us forever, that will still be there when we reveal the hidden parts of ourselves; a love that will endure in good times or bad, for better or worse. When we get married, we expect that from our husbands.

I remember one time, early in our marriage, when we were hanging a heavy picture on the wall. In our ignorance we hung it on a nail. The picture and nail came crashing to the floor. It should have been pretty obvious that the nail would not be strong enough to hold the picture's weight, but we had never heard of toggle bolts. We thought nails could hold anything.

In the same way human love, however beautiful, is not strong enough to support the full weight of a person's need for love. Human love can provide an exquisite taste of closeness to another and the warm companionship of a special person at our side, but only God's love can sustain us and carry us over the rough places that life throws in our path.

When we depend solely on our husband's love for happiness, security, or a feeling of self-worth, a time may come when the unintended pressure on the relationship causes deep fissures. It may even cause collapse. Humans are frail creatures. Sin clouds our eyes and sinks its tentacles down into our hearts. It warps our perspective and tarnishes the strength of our intentions. The frail human sin nature can contaminate even the most ideal human love.

In contrast, God's loving arms long to hold us in safety and security even in our weakest moments. His arms are strong. They never tire. Our tears never wear him down. Our pleas do not go unnoticed. Our PMS doesn't unnerve him. When our hair is frizzy and our makeup has worn off, he doesn't care; he loves us anyway. When the pounds layer on our hips, he sees only the beauty that lies within. When the lines of our face deepen and gray streaks our hair, he smiles that we are that much closer to our heavenly abode with him.

Your value does not depend on your husband's treatment or opinion of you. Your husband is a fallible human being carrying around a sinful nature. God is the one who gives you value. He also will give you a purpose, a hope, and a future. Do not look at yourself through your husband's eyes but through the eyes of God. You are precious to him. He loves you enough to let you think your own thoughts, feel your own feelings, have your own opinions, and be yourself. He loves you just the way you are. He created you with unique qualities, and he will never change his mind about you.

God's love is unconditional. His Son died for you when you were in your most sinful state. His deep, sacrificial love stretches through time to bring you to himself. The God who created the universe has chosen you as his special child, and he loves you with an unfailing and everlasting love. If the powerful God of the universe is for us, who can be against us?

Dear God, I am overwhelmed at the depth of your love, a love that never leaves and never gives up. God, let me lean into your love and feel the strength of your everlasting arms. When I am weak, sustain me. When I am discouraged, hold me up.

WITHDRAWAL

Each heart knows its own bitterness,
and no one else can share its joy.

—PROVERBS 14:10

At the edge of a desert landscape, I stood looking out over a brilliant blanket of golden California poppies, their bright petals outstretched in small circles of radiance to soak in the sun. Stepping out into the expansive field of wild-flowers, I began to snap pictures, enjoying the lovely canvas of orange, gold, and yellow. As the sun began its descent in the western sky, a chill began to stir the air. I made my way back to the car but turned around for another look just in time to see the scene changing before my eyes. The petals of the poppies were curling inward, closing up as if to protect themselves from the approaching darkness. In minutes all the cup-shaped flow-ers had hidden their bright faces from the gathering night.

One morning I sat in church thinking about the upcoming week, when I would travel to Birmingham for my daughter's graduation. My husband was going too. What would happen between us? I had seen him only once in the past four months. My heart was heavy with confusion and woundedness. My spirit drooped with fatigue.

When the congregation rose to sing, the people around me joined in celebration of song and praise to the Lord. But I just stood, barely mouthing the words of praise. Then I thought of the poppies. I remembered how they had folded up into them-selves as shades of evening approached. And I saw myself as one of the poppies.

I had folded my bright petals up into myself that morning. Even as I stood amid the joyous singing around me, all I could see, feel, or hear were the private feelings locked inside. I was shutting out the world. But, unlike the poppies that closed in response to the darkness, I was choosing to close up in the midst of God's sunshine. I was so buried in my own thoughts that I couldn't discern the difference between outside forces that hurt and those that heal. I had allowed myself to focus on my hurt rather than open my heart up to God.

Isn't that how we are sometimes? A friend puts an arm around us to help us feel better. A pastor preaches very real words of encouragement. Joyful music seeks to find an opening in our hearts. But we bury ourselves in our little world of pain and shut out the rest of the world, stubbornly refusing to release the buried feelings within. We don't seem to have the emotional, mental, or volitional strength to open up to the healing that is available. And the longer we shut ourselves up, the more clouded our thinking becomes, until the whole world seems utterly dark and hopeless.

At such a time you may not be able to praise God outright, but perhaps you can whisper, "I know I need you, God. I can't even say I want you right now, God, but I know if I open myself up, I will want you. Right now I'm hurting. Be my hiding place, God. I'll give up my hiding place here inside myself for the hiding place that is in you if you will quietly fold me in your arms. First let me hide myself in you. Then maybe I can open myself up to you."

> *You are my hiding place; you will protect*
> *me from trouble and surround me*
> *with songs of deliverance.*
>
> —Psalm 32:7

> *You are my fortress, my refuge in times of trouble.*
> —Psalm 59:16

WHERE DO I BEGIN?

*I am the way and the truth and the life. No one
comes to the Father except through me.*

—JOHN 14:6

*I*t was my turn to pick a hiking trail. All week my cousins and
I had been exploring new trails in the North Carolina
mountains, and when they suggested I choose one, I was determined to make it good. After looking through descriptions of the
various possibilities in the trail guide, I found a rugged one that
purportedly led to a beautiful view at the top of a mountain.

The eight of us probed the bushes at the bottom of the des-
ignated hill and, after a significant time, still could not find
where the trail began. Finally, one cousin uncovered what
appeared to be an overgrown path, and with a spirit of adven-
ture, bravado, and humor, we set out to follow it with hopes our
quest would not be in vain. After a short time, however, the path
disappeared into the woods, and we found ourselves deep in a
thicket of underbrush. Undaunted, several of us forked off what
was left of the path, exploring the possibility that it might continue at a farther point, but we only managed to uncover faint
traces of a trail's earlier existence. All day we wandered through
the woods on the side of the hill until we finally arrived at the
top, only to find a dense clump of trees blocking the view. In desperation one cousin climbed a tree to check out the promised
vista, but even from there he could see nothing. From that day to
this they tease me about my ability to pick trails.

The problem we had, of course, was that we never found
where the trail began—if the trail existed at all.

Sometimes life is like that: We aren't successful in achiev-
ing a goal because we don't know where to start. This can happen when traveling on a spiritual journey as well. We may feel
as though we are meandering all over, trying to find God, but

the real problem is that we haven't found where the path actually begins.

The path to God begins with making a decision of faith. You and I are looking for peace and hope, and we know God holds the key. But to find God and the treasures he offers, we must start with Jesus. Jesus is the path God has provided to himself.

Start at the point of realizing God's love for you. One of the incomprehensible truths of eternity is how the powerful God who created the universe can love imperfect people like you and me. But he does. In fact, one of the great themes of the Bible is God's constant seeking of a relationship with his people. We continually see God reaching out to humanity and humans turning their backs on God to go their own way in their sinful state.

God understood our weakness—that we could never be good enough, could never follow his laws. So in his mercy and love, he created a bridge between his own perfection and our failures so we would not have to miss the glorious eternity he has prepared for us. God allowed his Son, Jesus, to experience the death we deserve, and then to shed his death like a discarded garment and rise again into life so that we—despite our sin—could have a relationship with God. If you are ready to begin the journey and accept Jesus into your life, you will unleash one of the mysteries of God. When you give him your weakness, he makes his strength available to you.

> Dear Lord, I believe that you gave your Son, Jesus, to die for me and my sins. I thank you for your love and forgiveness, and I accept the incredible sacrifice that you made on the cross so I could have eternal life. God, I accept you as my Savior and Lord. I want to live for you. I give you my life and ask you to make me into the person you want me to be. Amen.

LETTING GO

Cast all your anxiety on him because he cares for you.
— 1 PETER 5:7

Strains from a familiar tune floated from the piano in the living room. My daughter Julie was playing a song we had often sung at church. I knew the words to "He Is Able" by heart, but they had never stayed in my heart like they did now. The soft tones began with the solid, reassuring refrain of the title that reminded me God could indeed accomplish whatever I was concerned about. The melody then soared into a bright crescendo of hope to affirm God's ability to do even more than I could imagine.

The song buoyed up my heart and sustained me for the rest of the day. It was a gentle reminder of God's sovereignty and power, which I needed to hear often to help me let go so God could do what I knew he alone could do.

In my dark valley of uncertainty, I was tempted to hold on to worry and fear as if they were old, sad friends. In some odd way, running back to those morose emotions produced a subconscious security, a subtle reassurance that I still had at least that much of a tie to my husband. But God wanted me to trust him enough to put my husband, my future, and all my worries into his hands. If I believed God cared for me and wanted the best for me, then why was I so fearful? The fact that I was worried proved I was not trusting God.

If you examine your heart, you may find that you, too, harbor a subconscious fear that by letting go of worry, you will also completely lose the man who shared your life. Even though the distance between him and you is huge, this dark thread of worry represents a reassuring connection. This is one of those times when spiritual truth flies in the face of logic, for if you are ever again to have him by your side, you must let him go emotionally.

Worry and fear block us from putting our complete trust in God, which in turn prevents God from pouring the full power of his resurrection grace into our circumstances. It is only in our letting go that God is able to bring to pass all that he purposes to do. Matthew 16:19 says, "Whatever you bind on earth will be bound in heaven, and whatever you loose on earth will be loosed in heaven." Our worry binds up God's freedom to complete his work. If we want God's best for our future, we must release the situation to him.

Perhaps our real fear is that God's intended outcome is not the same as ours. With enough worry we think we'll figure out a way to make things go the way we want. In our finite minds our plans seem better than God's. We can look with awesome wonder at the majesty of the universe he created but doubt his ability to bring good into our individual lives when we stand on the precipice of crisis.

God has a purpose and plan for each of us. He can bring beauty from ashes and gladness from mourning (Isa. 61:3). He makes all things work together for good to those who love him and are called according to his purpose (Rom. 8:28). He promises that he has plans to prosper us and not to harm us, plans to give us hope and a future (Jer. 29:11).

Trust him. Give him control of the reins. Let go of your worry and fear. He is able to do what you cannot do. And if you give it all to him, allowing him to carry that heavy load, he will give you peace and rest while he works out all the details.

Today, meditate on a Scripture. Choose one of your favorites from this book or from my Web site, www.brokenheartonhold.com, to post on the wall. When fear rises up or you are tempted to worry, fix your eyes and mind on a promise from God until your worry melts away and you can focus on the Lord once again.

Come to me, all you who are weary and
burdened, and I will give you rest.
—MATTHEW 11:28

TIME CAN BE YOUR FRIEND

*They that wait upon the LORD shall renew their
strength; they shall mount up with wings as eagles.*

—ISAIAH 40:31 KJV

*B*ecause your emotions are so turbulent, you may think no
happy answer to your situation is possible. Your thoughts
may run the gamut from a fairy-tale ending to the worst possible
outcome. When you find yourself in this state for very long, you
may be tempted to do whatever will give a clean resolution. You
want closure, even if that means doing what you really don't want
to do. But making rash decisions may be something you will woe-
fully regret later. Time may be your friend, if you let it.

When this disaster first swooped down upon me, my friend
Toni Jo said something that shocked me at first. I didn't want
to hear it.

"Don't be in a hurry," she said. "Give him as much time as
he needs. He's confused and needs to figure himself out. Tell
him to take a year if he needs it to figure out what he wants."

"A year!" I exclaimed. "A year?"

"What's a year in a whole lifetime?" she asked. "If it takes a
year for him to figure things out, and then you have thirty
more happy years together after that, wouldn't it be worth it?"

As it turned out, it took three years for my husband and me,
not one. But yes, it was worth it.

Trusting God includes waiting on him to do whatever he is
trying to do during this process. Because God does not force his
loving work into our lives, making rash decisions can preclude
God from accomplishing new dimensions of spiritual and emotional growth in you and your mate as well as others around
you. We need to give God time.

Waiting is extremely hard when each day weighs us down
with an eternity of suffering. But time has a way not only of
healing but also of giving perspective. What may seem true to

your mate today may look different to him tomorrow. Each new encounter between the two of you can set him or you off in a different relational direction, either positive or negative. Many years of clutter may need to go through the filter before the gemstones of your life together can become clear. If your husband has separated from you, he may be trying not to even think about you now. He may be focusing only on what he can make sense of. And that probably is not you and your relationship. Most likely he is filling his mind with work and other interests that keep him aloof emotionally.

During moments of deep depression, when you really want to give up, pick up your Bible and let God speak to you. Listen to what he says to you at that particular time. He wants to strengthen you, and you need strong wings if you're going to mount up on wings like eagles. Wait on the Lord. Remember, he is able to do more than we could ever imagine. But sometimes it requires time.

Lift your eyes and look to the heavens: Who created all these? He who brings out the starry host one by one, and calls them each by name. Because of his great power and mighty strength, not one of them is missing. Why do you say, O Jacob, and complain, O Israel, "My way is hidden from the LORD; my cause is disregarded by my God?" Do you not know? Have you not heard? The LORD is the everlasting God, the Creator of the ends of the earth. He will not grow tired or weary, and his understanding no one can fathom. He gives strength to the weary and increases the power of the weak. Even youths grow tired and weary, and young men stumble and fall; but those who hope in the LORD will renew their strength. They will soar on wings like eagles; they will run and not grow weary, they will walk and not be faint.

—ISAIAH 40:26–31

THE YEARS OF THE LOCUSTS

But even if I am being poured out like a drink
offering on the sacrifice and service coming from
your faith, I am glad and rejoice with all of you.
— PHILIPPIANS 2:17

*D*o you feel as though you've poured out your life like a sacrifice and now your cup is empty? Does it seem as though you have spent your life giving and giving, you've been there for everyone, and now you have nothing? Perhaps you are at a point in life where you see your children becoming increasingly independent and needing you less, just as you are also having to deal with the heartache of a husband who seems to have thrown you aside. Are you wondering what it has all been for?

At this moment the locusts appear to be eating away at the fruit of your life. As you look back over your years as wife and mother, you may feel you are looking at a barren piece of ground with little or nothing to show for all the labor and love given. But God promises to restore the years the locusts have eaten (Joel 2:25). Your faithfulness has not gone unnoticed by God. He will yet turn your mourning into gladness.

Vincent van Gogh died in 1890 fully believing he had been a complete failure as an artist. At the time of his death, it is believed that he had sold only a couple of paintings. Absolutely no value was placed on his work during his lifetime. However, in 1990 one of his paintings sold for $82.5 million. Furthermore, a whole museum in Amsterdam houses more than five hundred of his paintings and drawings. Had van Gogh accomplished anything in his life? Yes. Did he think so? No. Was he depressed? Yes. He was so depressed he cut off his own ear. What if he could have looked into the future and seen that one hundred years later a whole museum would be dedicated to his work and that someone would be willing to pay a fortune for one of his paintings? Would that have changed his perspective?

You may have invested your life in your family, and from the looks of it, all is for naught. But perhaps the beauty of what your efforts have produced will not truly be seen until a later time. God has promised to repay us for the years the locusts have eaten.

Don't be discouraged. Trust God. The future may hold treasures that are completely hidden from you now, but in God's perfect timing they will one day be revealed.

He will yet fill your mouth with
laughter and your lips with shouts of joy.
—Job 8:21

SEEING THE END FROM THE BEGINNING

I am the Alpha and the Omega, the First and the
Last, the Beginning and the End.
—Revelation 22:13

The beginning of a good book or movie often plops us down in the middle of a complicated plot, right in the thick of one of the most dramatic moments. We are held in suspense as we watch the protagonist face problems and make choices that propel the story along. We watch anxiously, hoping the protagonist makes her way through each obstacle. Because we are subconsciously aware of the fact that an author behind the scenes is driving the plot, we trust that by the end of the story all the events will line up and make sense. Typically, we have to read the end of the book, or see the end of the movie, before we fully understand what is happening at the beginning.

In these chaotic times when we don't have a clue what the end of this will look like, there is someone we can trust who is at both the beginning and the end of our story at the same time. God, the Alpha and Omega, is at the beginning and also at the end. As the plot of our story weaves through twists and tangles on its way to its conclusion, he is also in the middle. Only God can keep the plot on course and prevent one of the crisis points from overtaking the protagonist. He is in control. In this story you are the protagonist. God wants you to win. He wants you to push through the tangled plot and find victory at the other end.

Our part in this story is to trust the author/director as he shows us how to take the winding curves and travel the dark tunnels of the plot. As we take direction from him, he will give us the appropriate words and interactions with other players to successfully maneuver though the intrigue of the circumstances so the story comes out the way the author intends. His screenplay, with specific instructions and directions, is the Bible. And as the scenes unfold, he will be there personally to guide you through the action when you turn to him in prayer.

As in most good stories this one has a larger audience than just ourselves. Others are watching too. They are cheering for us to win, and will be horribly disappointed if we do not. And they are affected, not only by the outcome, but by the twists and turns of the plot itself ... and how we play our part.

What we do in the midst of these painful circumstances is one of the true tests of our Christian faith and can be one of the most beautiful testimonies of Christ's sustaining power that we can live out before our family and friends. This is your movie. Your life right now is the story. And you are the protagonist. Your audience is waiting to see how you, the protagonist, handle the crisis and find victory at the other end.

Seek first his kingdom and his righteousness, and
all these things will be given to you as well.
—MATTHEW 6:33

CHICKEN SOUP

Keep [my words] within your heart;
for they are life to those who find them and
health to a man's whole body.

—PROVERBS 4:21–22

The aroma of the chicken soup simmering in the pot tantalized my senses and drew me into the kitchen, where I breathed in the savory steam. My throat was dry and my nose swollen from a cold. As I began to ladle the soup into a bowl, the rich bouquet tugged at my insides with the promise of health even before the warm liquid touched my lips. I finished one bowl, then kept refilling it until the pot was empty. The very sinews of my body felt energized with new life.

On another day a family picture on the wall tore at my heart as I recalled happy times before chaos had disrupted our lives. My soul felt parched and dry. A deep hunger and thirst rose up within me and impelled me to open my Bible and thumb through the pages. At random I began to read. As words of Scripture soaked into my hungry soul, I wanted more. My thirsty spirit drank in verse after verse. As I continued to read, my body seemed to lap up the living water of God's Word, and new flesh formed on my dry bones.

When your rolling emotions will not subside and you cannot find peace; when your insides ache to be filled up; when you are hungry for love and comfort and nothing will satisfy, turn to God's Word. Let your thirsty soul drink in the living water from the pages of that eternal book. You may find it easier than usual to become absorbed in reading the Bible, and it may seem strange to you when you do not tire of it. But your soul is parched and wounded, and you need the healing and love that only God can give. Allow him to nurture you through his Word and pour his healing balm over your life.

If reading the Bible is hard for you, emotional and spiritual support can be found by listening to Bible teachers on the radio or television. A woman's Bible study or a worship experience may further your healing. Pick up Christian books to supplement your Bible reading, and listen to worship CDs to feed your heart.

By continuing to fill yourself with God's Word in these many forms, you will feed the hunger within. You will come to embrace God's peace that is beyond our finite understanding as its mystery is unlocked within your heart. And at the same time, you will find yourself growing in relationship to the Lord with a new tenderness and dependency that becomes sweeter as time goes by.

O dry bones, hear the word of the LORD.... I will put sinews on you, make flesh grow back on you, cover you with skin and put breath in you that you may come alive; and you will know that I am the LORD.

—Ezekiel 37:4–6 NASB

Keeping Your Focus

Blessed is the man [whose] ... delight is in the law of the LORD, and on his law he meditates day and night. He is like a tree planted by streams of water, which yields its fruit in season and whose leaf does not wither.

—Psalm 1:1–3

*J*t all depends on where my focus is." Those were my words to my counselor, Roger, as we discussed how I might relate to my estranged husband in the coming months. My husband and I had now been separated for almost two years. Roger was pleased that I had, so to speak, held out an olive branch to my husband so he could participate in planning our daughter's upcoming wedding. Prior to this conciliatory gesture I had fasted and prayed for a week, during which time I had laid my heart at the foot of God's throne as I kept my eyes fastened on Jesus. By asking God to take custody of my heart, rather than risking it once more to my husband, I was able to feel safe enough to invite my husband to join me in planning the wedding.

"I didn't detect any anger in you as you talked about being with him," Roger said, undoubtedly remembering how livid I had been the week before.

"Well, maybe not," I answered, "but the anger is right here and can take over any time. It just depends on where my focus is."

It was hard work continually focusing on the Lord. It was like having to exercise spiritual muscles. My mind so easily wandered off in one direction or the other, and my emotions always followed my thoughts. When my memory strayed back to words that had pierced my heart, whether said by my husband or others, depression and a feeling of hopelessness ensued. But when I spent an hour or more in the Bible, my thirsty heart drank in the living water and came to life again. I could see afresh with new eyes—with God's eyes. I could see that as I did not look to the right or to the left but only to him, my heart was ready to obey. I would once again retrieve my heart from the unsteady hand of my husband and trustingly put it in God's hands where I knew it would be tenderly and lovingly cared for.

God's purpose is to bring us close to him so that we can feel the security and sweetness of his love. He wants to teach us that he alone should be our focus. He wants to develop spiritual muscles in us that will keep us ever faithful to him, and as he does so, we become "like a tree planted by streams of water, which yields its fruit in season and whose leaf does not wither" (Ps. 1:3).

Lord, help me keep my eyes only on you. Steady me, Lord. Strengthen me.

THE BEACH BALL

*I call on the LORD in my distress,
and he answers me.*

—PSALM 120:1

The laughter of the children playing in the pool plucked away at the muggy afternoon heat, luring warm rays of sunshine into the tired places of my mind and spirit.

It was almost time to go home when one of the boys grabbed a beach ball from the pool deck and tossed it to another boy in the pool. A flurry of splashing and tussling ensued as the children scrambled for the ball, pushing one another under the water to grab for it. Then it was over. They climbed out of the pool. Their attention shifted to chomping on chips and toweling off as they headed into the house. The beach ball floated—forgotten—on the surface of the water.

For several days it bobbed about, buoyant and full of air. But as the days wore on, it started to deflate. Heavy and flat, it began to sink, drifting to the bottom of the pool, where it stayed until it was rescued days later.

Our emotions are like the beach ball floating around in a pool. When it is inflated, it floats on the top and bounces about and we experience life and peace. When it becomes deflated, it grows heavy and sinks to the bottom where depression and death engulf us. In times of grieving, our emotions, like the deflated beach ball, drop into pools of low resistance where dreadful memories and fears lurk. If depression sets in, we can become entirely engulfed in these heavy feelings unless we actively, forcefully, choose to set our mind on Jesus and let the Spirit take control.

Whenever you feel your emotions begin to sink, raise your eyes. Look to Jesus. Picture someone blowing up the deflated beach ball. In your mind watch the ball rise to the top. Then allow the Holy Spirit to breathe his Spirit into you. As you look to Jesus and feel the Spirit blow upon you, you will feel the depression fall away. You will know peace once again. And with that peace comes hope.

But if from there you seek the LORD your God,
you will find him if you look for him with all
your heart and with all your soul.
—DEUTERONOMY 4:29

THE PUZZLE

Trust in the LORD with all your
heart and lean not on your own understanding;
in all your ways acknowledge him, and
he will make your paths straight.
—PROVERBS 3:5–6

*P*icture a jigsaw puzzle emptied onto a table, all the pieces scattered about. No logical connection between the pieces seems to exist. Now picture an ant crawling onto one of the pieces. He sits on the puzzle piece without any idea as to what he is sitting on. It has splashes of color on it, but there is no picture. It seems meaningless. Then, as someone with intelligence and ability begins to put the pieces together, a picture begins to form. The pieces connect. The ant, too small to ever see that picture by himself, can see only one piece of the puzzle at a time. Even as the puzzle comes together, the ant can move from piece to piece but still cannot see the whole picture. He is too small and finite.

You are like that ant on the puzzle. Your understanding of what is happening is extremely limited. Everything is a jumble. You don't know how you got to where you are. You can't comprehend what is happening in your husband's mind, and you certainly don't know where you are going from here or how to proceed. You can see only the puzzle piece you stand on right now. You can't see the entire picture.

But God can. He puts the pieces together so they not only fit together perfectly but also create a beautiful, integrated design. And that is where trust comes in. Since we can't see the whole composition and God can, it only makes sense to trust the one who can see the picture that is taking form in the middle of our circumstances.

God knows both you and your husband. He sees the failures and shortcomings in both of you that brought you to this point. He knows what needs to be done to refine each of you into the man or woman he wants you to be so that you can enter into a deeper life with him and perhaps a new relationship with each other. He knows whether this is something that can be resolved quickly or if it is something that will take a long time. He is "the author and perfecter of our faith" (Heb. 12:2). No matter how much you mull over your situation, analyze yourself or your husband, read self-help books, talk to friends, or in other ways try to "understand" what is happening and how to resolve it, you will not find these things sufficient. They may enlighten you on various issues, but if you try to lean or depend on them, you will find yourself off balance or at the end of a dead-end road.

With all your heart, trust God to show the way. Whenever you feel yourself going off on some tangent, acknowledge him; seek his face. Ask God to direct your path and keep it straight.

Trust in the Lord with *all* your heart—not just a part of it, but *all* of it. Not even one little tiny corner should be *leaning on*—or depending on—your own understanding, for that one corner will pull you off center and away from the Lord. Our understanding is of the flesh, and "the mind set on the flesh is death, but the mind set on the Spirit is life and peace" (Rom. 8:6 NASB). Trust in the Lord, and when you hear yourself saying, "But what about ..." or "But I can't ...," realize you are beginning to lean on your own understanding.

"In *all* your ways acknowledge him." First, trust the Lord with *all your heart*; then *consciously* focus your *mind* on him. Don't let your thinking wander off into fearful or desperate speculations. He will "keep [you] in perfect peace, whose mind is stayed on [him]" (Isa. 26:3 RSV). Remember, God has this all under control. He knows the way. He is the master architect, the only wise God, our divine Creator. When the puzzle pieces of your circumstances finally connect, you will be able to look back and see the beautiful design God created.

> I can't see, Lord. But you can. When I look, all I see is the debris lying at my feet from the chaos of my life. But you can see. So as one who is blind, I will trust you to lead me through the rubble of my present circumstances out into the clear meadow of springtime.

All Things New

Let the morning bring me word of your unfailing
love, for I have put my trust in you.

—Psalm 143:8

The lights of the approaching cars blurred as Todd's head pounded. Although his eyes were fastened on the road ahead, his mind felt like a wrestling ring as his thoughts thrashed about, fighting against each other. Should he keep his appointment with the lawyer the next morning? Or were his friends right? Could Jill actually come to love him again? He couldn't imagine it. No. It was hopeless. Jill had told him she didn't love him. That was all there was to it. It was over.

"Feelings can change, Todd. Just because Jill feels this way today doesn't mean she'll feel this way tomorrow." The words Marion, a friend's wife, had said earlier that evening caused him to once again doubt the course of action he'd set in motion. Marion obviously believed it to be true.

But how could it be? He'd blown his relationship with Jill with his controlling ways and fierce temper. At first he had resisted Jill's accusations about his overbearing attitude, which had led to her leaving. But gradually he began to see that she was right, and he worked hard to change.

But it wasn't enough. Jill said she wanted a divorce. He wanted to finally do what she wanted. Giving her a divorce would be the kindest thing he could do for her.

Feelings can change, Todd....

He thought about the story Jim and Marion had told him about their marriage. They'd been separated for years and been through a really rough time. But now they were back together. And they were happy. Because they'd gone through their own dark tunnel—and come out the other side—they could see a light at the end of *his* tunnel, even if he couldn't see it.

Just because Jill feels this way today doesn't mean she'll feel this way tomorrow.

The encouragement in the words was hard to ignore. He wanted so much to believe it. But could he?

Holding onto a hope he couldn't see, the next morning he canceled his appointment with the lawyer and wrote Jill a letter. "I love you," he said. "I know I've wronged you, but I love you and want to stay married. If you want to get a divorce, I won't fight you. But I'm not going to initiate it. Do what you have to do."

The following night she came over to talk. That conversation led to two more in the next few days. A week later she moved back home. They still had much work to do to completely heal their marriage, but they had made it over the first big hurdle.

A new day and a new encounter can bring a new opportunity to turn things around. What was true yesterday may not be true tomorrow. God can turn things inside out when we put our hope in him. But as we place our hope in God and look into the face of Jesus, we need to also listen to his words. Sometimes his words of gentleness will soothe our hearts, but other times his words may pierce us with a sudden realization. At those times if we let his words sink down into the steely chambers of our heart, we may see a new direction he wants to take us in, a change in the attitude of our mind.

When my husband and I first separated, pastoral counselor Dick Moulton intrigued me with his notion that when couples come to him talking about divorce, they don't seem to really want to divorce the *person* in the marriage; they want to divorce the *form* of the marriage.

What does that mean? How can we change the *form* of our marriages?

Psychologists Barry Duncan and Joseph Rock, in their book *Overcoming Relationship Impasses* (Insight, 1991), talk about causal circles in relationships. "If one person in a couple changes his or her behavior noticeably and consistently, the other person's reactions will change, which will [then] change the first person's reaction."

The changes can be made in words or actions. Everything you do or don't do sends a message to your partner. It is a day-to-day walk. Yesterday has fallen apart, and the unfinished image of tomorrow is still forming in your two hearts, taking shape in the hands of God.

But as you look into the mirror of God's word and listen to his voice, you may see a new image of yourself, a new person he wants you to become. You may see blemishes he wants to peel away. And if you allow your heart to open up to his correction, you may find that subtle changes in yourself can steer your future in new directions and happier endings.

> God, show me how to change, what I can do to alter the course of my relationship with my spouse. Lord, I'm willing to become the new person you want me to be. I'm willing to listen. Give me the patience and diligence to follow through on what you teach me. Let me be a willing and active participant as you work in my marriage to make all things new.

BEFORE ALL THE WORLD

*T*he shrill ringing of the telephone cut through the prattle of children's voices. Penny and her four children were having lunch around the long table in the great room during a break from homeschooling.

"I'll get it," Penny said to her thirteen-year-old son, who was turning in his chair looking toward the sound. "You go ahead and eat. You need to get back to your schoolwork."

Penny reached for the phone and heard her husband Nick's low, resonant voice on the other end.

"Penny," he said, "I'm in jail."

Penny's throat tightened. *Jail?* She looked at the children.

"I need you to come down here with some money." His voice sounded far away like in a dream.

Jail? Nick in jail? A picture of him bouncing their youngest child on his lap flitted through her mind. She saw his face as it appeared on the TV screen every night. He was the news anchor on the local TV station. He was a Christian who was vocal in his testimony. *Jail?*

"What have you done, Nick?" she heard her voice magnified with the intensity of the emotions rising within her.

He didn't answer. Instead, he said, "You just need to come down here right now."

Into the fog of her mind rose the words from her random Bible reading with her two older sons that morning. *No.* She pushed it from her mind. *No.*

But the thought persisted.

The Scripture verse that morning had seemed inconsequential, just the next verse in the chapter, one to get through so they could get to one more relevant. First Corinthians 6:15. What did that have to do with anything? She couldn't shake it from her mind: "Shall I then take the members of Christ and unite them with a prostitute?"

Something inside prodded her. Finally she asked, "Does this have anything to do with prostitution?"

He hesitated. She sensed his surprise at the other end.

"Yes," he said.

Penny felt the blood drain from her body. Her mind went numb. She stared at the table but was no longer looking at the children. Her eyes glazed over. "I'm not going to be able to come down and get you," she said, her voice flat and lifeless. "You're going to have to call your mom and dad."

She replaced the phone and stood there feeling cold, weightless, as though she were going to faint. The two older boys at the table watched her, listening. Somewhere in her subconscious state she saw their eyes fastened on her. But she couldn't move. The younger ones, oblivious, began to play with the toys strewn over the floor.

Her mind was spinning. What was happening? She couldn't comprehend the reality of what she'd just heard. Her husband—strong in his faith, respected as a wholesome family man with high moral values. A man who modeled his Christianity before the whole community in a high-profile position. *Prostitution.* What would she do? The diseases he could transmit to her. She covered her face with her hands, dropped them down again, then groped for a chair. How could he do this to her? *Arrested for having sex with a prostitute!* The horror of it ravaged her mind.

For the next few hours Penny walked around in a trance, the bubble of her world bursting around her. Marriage and family had been everything. How could she trust her life any more?

Her older boys were watching. She knew they'd heard. What could she say to them? What would they think? "We'll get through this," she said, attempting to pull herself from her state of confusion. She looked at them and felt her heart sink in discouragement and pain. All the noble things she and her husband had tried to teach their children—gone.

"We need to pray," she said. "It'll be okay." Then she picked up the phone and called the one person she felt would understand and help her focus.

Sandy was a woman whose own marriage breakup had only strengthened her belief in the sanctity of marriage. She did understand, but she also assured Penny that forgiveness was possible, an idea Penny found completely repugnant.

"No way," Penny said.

"Think of the children," Sandy said. "It will be worth it. And you can do it. It's not easy, but you can do it."

The rest of the day was a fog. Penny cried out to God while Nick's offense flared in graphic, psychedelic images before her eyes and Sandy's challenging words rolled around inside her head. What would she do when Nick came home? There was no way she could forgive him. Anger churned within her.

"We gotta talk," she said when Nick dragged himself through the front door that evening. Her body felt tense; her fingers clenched in a ball. When they had slipped into the bedroom and closed the door, she faced him squarely. "What happened?" she asked sternly.

Through eyes of anger, she looked for the familiar cocky lift of his shoulders, the defiant stubbornness of his raised chin. He would be afraid for his job—for his reputation. It would get out in the news. Did he realize what he'd done to *her?* To the *children?* If his career was his primary concern—she didn't think she could hang on. She couldn't take it. It was too excruciating.

But the proud reactions she expected were not there. He hung his head, his face pale, a look of hopelessness stealing the light from his eyes. He was broken. Devastated.

"Well?" she repeated. "What happened?" But as the words left her mouth, she saw him—really saw him. He looked back at her with a look of desperation and groped for words of remorse and apology.

"I'm sorry, Penny," he said pressing his fingers against his forehead and jamming them through the shock of thick brown hair. "I'm so sorry. I know what I did was awful. I love you—and I love the children. I don't want to lose you. I'm sorry." Tears welled in his eyes. "All this—fame. It goes to your head. You're treated like you're something really special. It's hard to handle. But all that is nothing. It's you and the kids I don't want to lose." He sat on the end of the bed and buried his face in his hands.

Penny stood to leave the room, then turned to him without a trace of warmth. "I won't leave you alone with this," she said. There was a pleading look in his eyes as he looked up at her. A sliver of compassion mingled with the anger that seared her heart. Nick looked so awful. He was contrite. He was rock bottom. She sensed his panic. She was almost afraid of what he might do if she abandoned him now. "I love you, and I want to see this through with you," she said. But her heart churned even as she said the words. How would she do it? How would she see it through with him?

Their pastor called at 10:00 p.m.

"Sandy called me and told me what happened," he said. "Is it okay if I come over?"

In the late hours of the night, they sat around the table of the great room listening to their pastor's counsel. He didn't mince words.

Pride had gone to Nick's head, he said. Ambition had ruled his heart. And with a sense of self-importance he had cast aside his caution, allowing his desires to overpower him. And in the vacuum, lust gained a stronghold. The pastor even suggested that Nick consider quitting his job.

Nick stared at him thoughtfully, then nodded. "Yes," he said. "You're right." As much as he loved his job as a newscaster, he didn't even wince. "I'll do what you say."

Penny was stunned. *Give up his job? The job he had worked so hard to get?* Nick was so pliable, so repentant. He wasn't even questioning their pastor's counsel. The doubts racing around in her mind found an anchor of truth to cling to. Seeing the sincerity of his heart calmed her fears.

But another fear nagged at her heart—the inevitability of the media discovering a juicy scandal. They would be the butt of ridicule and derision. People would mock them for their professed Christian morality—even worse, Nick's shame would sully the very name of Christ. Penny hardly slept as she and Nick waited for the inevitable phone call. However, during the next few days, they spent many hours talking together as their pastor had advised. For the first time in their marriage, they honestly shared their innermost struggles. The intensity of their openness was painful as she and Nick each revealed deep thoughts and concerns about one another.

"Have you used a prostitute before?" Penny asked.

"Yes," he admitted honestly. It was a devastating blow. But through it all, a new understanding and closeness began to grow between them. It was a unity they needed in order to face the coming days.

Nick answered the phone one afternoon to a reporter's mocking voice. "Gotcha," she said. "I read the reports."

"Yeah, I thought you would," he said, refusing to be evasive. "I'm extremely sorry about everything."

"How will this affect your job?"

"My primary concern is my family, but I know I have sinned against God, my wife, my children, and the audience I serve."

The story was on the front page of the hometown newspaper the following day. At a press conference later in the week,

Nick stood before a podium in his best suit, trying to hide his humiliation. His face was contrite. His words humble. He again repented of his sin and declared his intention to resign from his public position. Nick and Penny hoped his forthrightness would end the public face of their private pain. But it didn't.

The following day, when Penny opened the front door, camera lights blazed, reporters waited. Quickly slamming the door, she leaned back against it. She was trembling. Taking a deep breath, she went in to the children. "How would you like to go to some of your friends' houses today?"

When she returned later, the media were still camped out at their front door.

It was the next Sunday, at the end of the morning church service, when their wounds of heartache, isolation, and shame began to heal. Asking Nick and Penny to stand, their pastor turned to the congregation. "I'm sure you've all seen the papers," he said. "I've spent hours talking with Nick, and he realizes it was out of God's discipline and love that his sin was exposed. We as a church are now in the process of restoration for Nick and his family." When the pastor and members gathered around them to pray, Penny felt God's comfort surround her. Without whitewashing Nick's offense, the congregation fully embraced them.

In the weeks that followed, Penny and Nick worked to restore their family, while simultaneously struggling to keep the media at bay. When a major national news program called, they left town for a long weekend. Nick spent hours with his older boys laying his heart before them in honesty and humility as he shared the truth of God's Word.

Their church became a place of refuge in the confusion that surrounded them. They attended Bible studies and home groups. Nick went to counseling, then joined a men's accountability group. He dealt with the pride and ambition that had gone to his head, and he became accountable to his group and to Penny for the lust that had become a stumbling block. They received encouraging letters from scores of Christians.

On her part, Penny took to heart the counsel of her pastor, who warned her against self-righteousness and slander of her husband. They used the time as a window of opportunity to be open with one another, and Nick became more affectionate and attentive to her and the children.

Although it was a painful period neither would want to repeat, several years later, Penny and Nick have a stronger marriage than before. They prize their time together and with the family beyond anything else. Their communication has become far more real, and they always remain in touch now even when physically apart. Together they have grown closer to God, who is the source of the love and forgiveness they share with one another. While still in their early twenties, their two older boys made a pledge of sexual purity until marriage.

Whenever Penny and Nick have doubts or struggle with what lies ahead, they take hold of Philippians 1:6: "He who began a good work in you will carry it on to completion until the day of Christ Jesus." All they have to do is look back to see the work God did in their own lives a number of years ago to see God's faithfulness and goodness for the future.

Part 3

SEARCHING YOUR HEART

Search me, O God, and know my heart;
test me and know my thoughts.
See if there is any wicked way in me, and
lead me in the way everlasting.
—PSALM 139:23–24 NRSV

MIGRATING SOUTH

How long, O LORD? Will you forget me forever?
How long will you hide your face from me?
How long must I wrestle with my thoughts
and every day have sorrow in my heart? ...
Look on me and answer, O LORD my God.

—PSALM 13:1-3

*M*y fingers felt icy and stiff as they curled about the steering wheel on that cold December morning. Ahead of me I envisioned another bleak day at the office, with my heart neither alive nor fully dead, one more day when life would illusively move in slow motion just beyond my reach.

As I stared blankly before me, I noticed an apparition of white coming into view at the top of my windshield, cruising ahead of me in the sky above. Curiously crooking my head to look up through the top of the windshield, I saw a flock of migrating birds. Hundreds of them flew together in a perfect V, each bird in concert with the others, beautifully unified in their common course. I watched enviously as the birds sailed swiftly overhead, pointing confidently toward their destination.

Like the birds seeking a warmer climate, something in me innately sought comfort. I wanted to escape from my heartache, to fly south with the birds, to find a safe haven where pain could not penetrate. It seemed unnatural to willingly stay in a place that brought suffering. But deep within me I knew I must stay exactly where I was and live out each day. For sometimes by design, God allows us to stay in a situation of distress and discomfort because he sees it as a place where we can grow.

As I looked into the future, I recognized the awful reality of my suffering: It would be with me during this time no matter what I did. I had never known such agony. This was not supposed to happen. I didn't understand.

But gradually God unfolded to me a deeper reality. What I was experiencing was not just about me; nor was it just about my husband and me ... or our marriage. It was about a picture God was composing even as I stood poised on the tip of his paintbrush spilling tears upon the canvas to soften the harsh colors of the palette.

As I spent time with him in prayer, his larger purpose began to take form before my eyes. This grievous time was only one part of God's bigger picture. What this part of the picture would ultimately look like, however, depended in large part on me and what I did with my circumstances. It could be an obscure, narrow section angled awkwardly among the other images on the canvas. Or it could become a shining blast of color and light shedding rays of illumination on the surrounding landscape. It was up to me to seek and find his larger design.

What did God want to show me? What did God want me to do? Even as I spent time with him in prayer, earnestly seeking, I could only see dim images in my mind. The dark tunnel moved on with only intermittent flickers of light to give me hope. I began to realize that if I wanted to see the picture, if I wanted to reach the world outside and know the light of joy, there was only one way out. But I had to choose it. In this tunnel of darkness, I could either walk out of it day by day, slowly, with Jesus or stay trapped within while continuing to try new maneuvers on my own. My only real hope was to keep pressing on, trusting God, taking one step at a time. He knew the way out into the light. He could lead the way. But I needed to give him time.

When you abide with God during this time, his message eventually becomes a living, palpable, heartfelt reality. As one of his truths penetrates beneath the heartache, your pain becomes a seed, dying in the soil of your heart and sprouting roots that in time produce something new and beautiful, bearing a fruit whose taste is sweet and whose fragrance invites others to God's throne.

God, hold me close as I trust you to guide me through this dark tunnel. I know that only by leaning on you will I ever make it to the other side. Give me the will to hold on and the faith to do it your way. Let me become a sweet aroma to you and others as you bring beauty from my awful pain.

GOING DEEPER

But if from there you seek the LORD your God, you will find him if you look for him with all your heart and with all your soul.

—DEUTERONOMY 4:29

T he first time I remember ever really thinking about the idea of going deeper in the Christian life was one night in church a year before my separation. I had gone alone that evening, and a feeling of desperation had begun to gnaw at my insides. I felt my marriage unraveling. Something was wrong, and I didn't know what it was. Arguments were more heated and arbitrary. I was losing my sense of who my husband was.

I cannot remember what the sermon was about that evening except that at some point my pastor said, "If things are not working out in normal ways, if you're trying to live by the old rules that used to work, but they're not working anymore, then maybe it's time to go deeper."

As I left the church, my heart was numb. Why was my husband gone so much? Why was he so angry? I stopped by some friends' house on the way home and asked them to pray for our marriage. But those words stuck with me: *"Maybe it's time to go deeper."*

Going deeper—what did that mean? I knew all about being a good Christian. I felt pretty good about keeping the commandments and following the rules. I went to church, read the Bible, prayed. I had my theology all figured out. I had no idea there was another whole dimension.

The rich young ruler in Matthew 19 was like that. He followed all the commandments from his youth and earnestly desired to follow Christ. But he could not comprehend a dimension beyond the earthly security of his wealth. So he walked away.

When the security and stability of our marriages are crumbling before our eyes, however, we are in a different position than the rich young ruler. Our lives aren't secure. We have already been stricken. The senselessness of our circumstances has moved us from a world of cause and effect to a world where gravity no longer seems to hold our feet to the ground and law and order don't work. The plans we make are moonbeams in our hands. It is as though we are thrown into the weightlessness of a time capsule, like astronauts living in an out-of-control environment.

Going deeper in the Christian life can begin by humbling yourself as a little child and holding onto the hand of the Father so he can lead you through the darkness. Then, as you listen for his voice in the silence, you will feel his closeness and discover a deeper reality you never knew was there. When you reach into the dark ahead of you, you will be greeted not by the emptiness of being alone, but by the warm touch of your Savior walking beside you leading you onward.

But there is so much more. Romans 8:28 tells us, "In all things God works for the good of those who love him, who have been called according to his purpose." If you can be still before God, relinquish your own willfulness, and accept this promise, then God will lift you above your own faint understanding of life so you can become a part of his larger story.

Romans 8:29 says, "For those God foreknew he also predestined to be conformed to the likeness of his Son." Part of God's plan is to give us eyes to see beyond the finite habitat of this world so we can see him more clearly through his Word. As we do so, we will have an increasing desire to live in the light of his presence and be more like him. In the mirror of his Word, he convicts us of our own shabbiness so that eventually we surrender to his will and allow him to replace the rags of our meager righteousness with the splendor of his incredible goodness.

*Therefore, I urge you, brothers, in view of God's mercy,
to offer your bodies as living sacrifices, holy and pleasing to God—this is your spiritual act of worship. Do
not conform any longer to the pattern of this world, but
be transformed by the renewing of your mind. Then
you will be able to test and approve what God's will
is—his good, pleasing and perfect will. For by the grace
given me I say to every one of you: Do not think of
yourself more highly than you ought, but rather think
of yourself with sober judgment, in accordance with the
measure of faith God has given you.*

—ROMANS 12:1–3

SEEING WITH NEW EYES

*Search me, O God, and know my heart;
test me and know my thoughts.
See if there is any wicked way in me, and
lead me in the way everlasting.*

—PSALM 139:23–24 NRSV

I awoke with a start. Something new was pulsating
through my mind. A new thought. A strange fear.
Something I couldn't identify. I looked over at the clock; it was
3:30 a.m. An uneasiness that had followed me to bed had ger-
minated as I tried to sleep. It was as though scales were falling
from my eyes. Even though the only light in the room
emanated from the fluorescent dial on the clock, I saw everything clearly, as though for the first time. *It wasn't all his fault.*
I was seized with conviction.

The evening before, I had sat forlornly beside my mother-in-law, bitterly pouring out my pain. Through the years she and I had become very close. I knew she cared for me almost as a daughter and that she was suffering tremendously over my separation from her son. Although her words were gentle and supportive, somewhere in her eyes I sensed a pleading question, as if she were saying, *Yes, I see your side. You have a right to be upset, but isn't there some fault on your side too?*

Now last night was only a dim memory. What leapt up blatantly before my eyes was a picture of myself I didn't like. With new eyes, I saw a Linda I had never seen before. I wanted to hide her somewhere and pretend she didn't exist. This new Linda stood before me exposed with all her warts and ugly attitudes. *It wasn't all his fault.* God had plopped this new Linda down in front of me in the middle of the night to show me I could no longer hide her. She, after all, was part of the problem. Throughout this crisis, I had seen my husband in black and me in white. But suddenly everything had changed.

I got up, turned on the light, and fumbled around on my desk for a pad of paper. Nervously I fingered a pen and began to write a letter to *him*. On those pages I poured out my heart, acknowledging what God was showing me, acknowledging that we were both sinners, both fallen, both responsible for what had happened to our marriage. I didn't absolve him from his wrong, but neither did I excuse myself. I asked him to forgive me for my part in the deterioration of our marriage. I recognized that perhaps it was too late. And I confessed that I didn't even know, at that moment, if I could ever become the wife he needed me to be. I told him I would pray for him and asked him to pray for me.

At some point along the way, we need to open our hearts to God in humility so he can show us our own part in this marital impasse. For some it may be a sin harbored deep within that negatively affected the marriage. For others it may be a fearful passiveness that kept us from asserting ourselves in healthy ways. Or it may be an unconscious negligence toward our husbands' needs.

Let God convict you of your part as you search the Scriptures today. Then record your thoughts in a journal. Sending a letter or even writing one should be done only if God specifically moves you in that direction. But as the Lord shows you your part in the failure of your marriage, lift the pain of self-knowledge and sin to God for his forgiveness and peace.

> Dear God, I know I share the blame for what has happened in my marriage. It's not all his fault. But it's so much easier to see his guilt than mine. Lord, open my eyes so I can see the hidden secrets that lie festering in the corners of my heart. Open my mind to the truth as I search the Scriptures today and in the days to come. When I see what I don't want to see, give me the strength to honestly face myself instead of making excuses. Then please, God, give me the courage and humility to lift my sin up to you in repentance so I can receive your forgiveness and the freshness of a clean heart.

All a man's ways seem innocent to him, but
motives are weighed by the LORD.
—PROVERBS 16:2

WEEDS

Let us throw off everything that hinders and
the sin that so easily entangles, and let
us run with perseverance the race marked
out for us. Let us fix our eyes on Jesus,
the author and perfecter of our faith.
—HEBREWS 12:1–2

As a would-be backyard gardener, I enjoy working outside in God's creation, trying to bring beauty and order out of the chaos of my yard. Sometimes, when a weed springs up next to a valuable plant, I find that its roots have not only grown deep but they also have become entangled among the roots of the plant I want to keep. Consequently, to pull the weed, I have to dig down and separate the bad roots from the good roots, which can be quite a delicate procedure. It may be hard to distinguish one from the other, and I have to be careful not to damage the good roots while identifying and pulling out the bad ones.

Perhaps there are sins in our lives or the lives of our husbands that resemble these weeds. These sins may have originated from our youth. Because they have been so long in our lives, their roots are deep and so enmeshed in our personalities that we aren't sure where the sin ends and our real personality begins.

These sins may have become coping mechanisms—such as anger, running away from problems, pride, a critical or controlling spirit, sarcasm, or self-pity. We may say, "Well, that's just the way I am." But actually it's just a sin we have become dependent on and may not want to face.

God may be saying, "I do not want that sin in your life. That sin has contributed to the problems in your marriage. And in your crisis, one of my purposes is to reach into your life and cut that sin out, to disentangle the roots of that sin from the real you I created you to be. I am the author and perfecter of your faith, and as you look to me, I want you to recognize that one of my roles in your life is to bring you to perfection."

If this is what God is doing in your life or your husband's life, it may take time. You may need to pray that God will give you the patience to wait as he slowly teaches you and your husband day by day what each of you individually need to learn.

> Lord, teach me your ways. Show me what I need to do to throw off the sin that is entangled in my life and that keeps me from being all you want me to be. Give me the

patience to wait for you to complete your
work in both my husband and me.

DETOURS

*If I rise on the wings of the dawn, if I settle on
the far side of the sea, even there your hand will
guide me, your right hand will hold me fast.*

—PSALM 139:9–10

 he traffic cop stood at the intersection, pointing us
toward a road to the right. Beyond him we saw mangled
cars strewn across the highway with ambulances angled among
them. We turned onto the detour to see that it was a narrow
street with only a single lane in either direction. Cars crawled
along ahead of us. This detour would cause a long delay in getting us to our hotel, and we feared losing our reservation.

When a detour interrupts a journey, it can be terribly incon-
venient. It may make you late. You may get lost. Similarly, as
you travel through life, a crisis looming up to block your way
sends you veering off your familiar and anticipated pathway. As
you wind through unmarked streets and alleys, you may feel
lost and afraid.

But if you look closely at the patrolman pointing the way,
you may find yourself looking into the face of God. This journey, though difficult, could indeed be one of God's divine
detours, prolonging your trip but helping you avoid a crash
with more serious consequences farther up the road.

I was surprised to discover in the story of Moses leading the
Hebrews out of Egypt in Exodus 13 and 14, that God intentionally led the people the long way *toward* the Red Sea instead of

going the shorter route through the Philistine country. God chose to take the Israelites on a detour on purpose. He may be doing the same with you.

God knew what the Hebrews did not know—that if they went the shorter way through the land of the Philistines, they would encounter a fierce enemy they were not prepared to fight. God knew they needed a period of strengthening and discipline before such a battle.

And when the detour led to an apparent dead end called the Red Sea, God knew beforehand what he would do. Although the people would be afraid, he wanted them to see his power and omnipotence and learn to trust him in the midst of fear. When they reached the Promised Land, they would have to fight giants. His detour was meant to strengthen their faith for the battle.

Your Red Sea may overwhelm you. You thought you were on a road with a sure destination, accompanied by a partner who was there for the duration. But God wants you to learn to trust him when facing detours in your life, to lean on him and look to him for direction and guidance. His purpose is to give you hope and a future. He knows where this detour will take you and at what point it will reconnect with the main road. He knows how long it will take and why it is necessary.

He wants to make you strong enough to withstand life's battles. He brought you into this journey, not to defeat *you* but to defeat the giants that are ahead. Your detour has a purpose. Trust God to lead you through it.

Lord, don't let me miss your purpose in this detour I am on. Help me to be teachable, pliable, patient, and ready to hear your voice. You know my anxiety and my fear. Right now I am choosing to place my trust in you. Give me the strength, Lord, to continue to trust you.

LOOKING FOR THE LIGHT

Who among you fears the Lord and obeys
his Servant? If such men walk in darkness,
without one ray of light, let them trust the
Lord, let them rely upon their God. But see
here, you who live in your own light, and
warm yourselves from your own fires and not
from God's; you will live among sorrows.

—ISAIAH 50:10–11 TLB

*W*hy must good people suffer? It is one of the most frequently asked questions about the character of God. It was Job's question as well as ours: "Your hands shaped me and made me. Will you now turn and destroy me?" (Job 10:8).

It's not hard to imagine how Job must have felt when he cried out, "If only my anguish could be weighed and all my misery be placed on the scales! It would surely outweigh the sand of the seas" (Job 6:2–3). We know about suffering—it has become our companion. Like a shadow that clings to our heart, it won't leave us alone. Wanting to escape from it, we try to manipulate it, cry out against it, yell at it. Just like Job, we grieve.

Embedded in the story of Job is the classic picture of a person struggling with pain and going through the grief process. We see Job sinking into the depths of depression, bemoaning that he was ever born, wanting to die. We see him striking out in anger as he challenges God to a trial. Later, we find him searching his past to see where he could have gone wrong, but he finds nothing to regret. Job was normal in the way he dealt with his suffering. Like you and me, he worked through the grief process looking for answers.

The Grief Process

Regardless of how your situation ends, the grief process is a natural part of your crisis. The stages of grief consist of denial, depression, anger, guilt, and acceptance. As you go through each stage, expect to cycle back through the others many times, sometimes within the very same day.

Denial, the first stage, begins with you feeling emotionally numb. You may deny the truth of what is happening or that it will have any effect on you. This phase may *feel* better, but only as your feelings come to the surface can you begin to heal.

Anger is the stage in which you will feel hostility toward your husband, family and friends who are unable to understand or help, God for letting this happen, or anyone else who might have contributed to the problem or seems to stand in the way of a solution. Physical exercise and journaling may prove helpful.

Depression may last the longest. Warning signs include restlessness, fatigue, inability to sleep or a desire to sleep too much, crying easily, wanting to withdraw, finding it hard to concentrate, forgetfulness, loss of appetite or a compulsion to overeat or drink, and a sense of helplessness or despair.

Consider talking out your feelings with a friend or counselor; set some short-term goals and stick with them; write in a journal; don't be afraid to cry; and pray. Though a period of depression is very normal, if symptoms persist, you may want to see a counselor.

Guilt is another normal part of grief, but be sure to distinguish between false guilt and true conviction. Friends or a counselor can help you address these issues realistically. A general feeling of condemnation—or false guilt—will incapacitate you, but an honest conviction will help you recognize specific offenses. Don't be too hard on yourself, but as you see areas of your life where you have made mistakes, let God move you from where you are into the future. Seek forgiveness where necessary, and make changes that can smooth out the path ahead. As you seek God's forgiveness, remember to forgive yourself as well.

Acceptance, the final stage, is when you are able to move ahead with hope and purpose.

Working Through the Pain

While Job experienced tremendous suffering, he never wavered in his faith or dishonored God through his actions. He asked questions and worked through his grief, but in the end he had a deeper relationship with God, and his blessings doubled.

At some point, each of us makes a decision to either stay stuck in one part of our grief or move on to eventual healing. If we don't work all the way through it, pain and suffering can take a tragic toll. If we internalize our pain, depression takes hold and we may seek unhealthy outlets of escape. If we become stuck in anger, we will lash out at God or others, looking for retribution. We may feel justified, but we will also reap a bitterness that eats us up inside.

But if we persist in working through our pain, then we, like Job, will be blessed in unexpected ways. God has not abandoned us, even though we may think he has. If we become discouraged and give up before God finishes his work, we are like the person looking at a cake in the oven before it is done. "I knew it wouldn't rise," we say. But we haven't given it time to become what it's supposed to be.

We may never completely understand the why—the reason for our suffering. Maybe, as with Job, it's a period of testing; maybe it's for discipline or growth. But whatever the reason, the fruit of holding on to God and surrendering our will and emotions to him while we wait in limbo will eventually bring incomparable peace and grace that only God can give.

Allow yourself the freedom to experience the different stages of grief. But know that God is there with you all the time. Look to him. Abide with him. He is the Light that shines in darkness and illuminates your path.

In all things God works for the good of those who love him, who have been called according to his purpose.
—ROMANS 8:28

NO PLACE TO GO

Be still, and know that I am God.

—PSALM 46:10

*J*oan slammed the phone down on the receiver, then flung herself on the couch, her chest heaving in sobs. *Why do I always do that? Why do I call him? I knew it was a mistake before I dialed the number.*

"I hate him," she screamed. "He's ruined my life."

She pictured her husband's face as his words sliced through her heart like a knife once again. "I don't love you," he'd said. "Don't you understand? I love Dana."

An hour earlier she had felt hopeful. She was coping. Now here she was again, falling apart. How could her husband leave her for another woman? How could this actually be happening? She desperately wanted to hope he would see the light—that he would realize how wrong he was before they met with the lawyers the following week. Surely she could convince him it was wrong.

"Don't call him, Joan. Pray for him, but don't pursue him. Give him space. Let God work on his heart."

Her friend Cynthia's advice was right. She shouldn't have called him. But what could she do?

Whatever the crisis that plagues your marriage, the feeling of abandonment causes a frenzy of emotion in search of answers. But there may come a time when all the paths have merged into one and there is no place else to go. You are on a moving walkway headed forward. You don't like where it's headed, but you're going there nonetheless. You feel forsaken by every trace of happiness and hope. It even seems like God has deserted you.

But he hasn't.

When your pain threatens to overrun you, stop for a few moments. Get alone, and ask God to come and "sit" with you while allowing yourself to simply feel. "Sitting in the pain," as

Job did, can help us acknowledge its depth, bring it to the surface, and eventually move us out of it toward healing. If you can, write your thoughts in a journal. Don't be afraid of their intensity, and don't be afraid to write exactly what goes through your mind. Acknowledging the reality of your situation is part of the grief process and will move you toward healing.

God knows your anguish, your anger, and your sadness, and he can carry these heavy emotions for you. Lamentations 3:57 says, "You came near when I called you, and you said, 'Do not fear.'" God is here. Don't be afraid.

> O God, I never imagined that I could hurt
> so much. Please come and sit with me; I
> need someone to help me bear this load.

HEALING LIPS

A wise man's heart guides his mouth,
and his lips promote instruction.

—PROVERBS 16:23

Eyes glued to the screen, I watched the characters in the movie *The First Wives Club* with interest and glee. How my heart applauded as Goldie Hawn, portraying a wife abandoned by her husband, flounced through her husband's office and house, stripping him of his most prized possessions as a look of dismay spread over his face. I giggled when she clunked two quarters onto his desk as his half of the assets after he forced her to dispose of their common property. And I smiled broadly as she and the other two rejected, distraught, and discarded wives linked arms and danced down the street, singing a song of freedom and emancipation from their unfaithful husbands.

Good for you, girls, I thought. I would never dream of doing the wild things they did. It was ludicrous; it was crazy—it was wonderful!

I watched the movie three times.

In our deep hurts our hearts ache for retribution. Our nerves bristle with the need for action. We want to retaliate, make a smart remark so he will know how much hurt he has caused. We are consumed with a desire for him to experience our pain. So we revel in a sarcastic comeback or a dramatic prank that might get his attention. We need catharsis. We need to release our anger.

One of the sad truths of human experience is that all too often we respond to the most important times in our life in a completely reckless fashion. The minute we hear his voice or see his face, the pain we feel rolls off our tongue in an anger that cries out to be expressed. And it should be expressed—at the right time, in the right setting, and in the right manner— just as God directed: "Be angry but do not sin" (Eph. 4:26 RSV).

"No man can tame the tongue," James 3:8 says. "It is a restless evil, full of deadly poison." Letting words roll off our tongues without restraint may feel good, but it will broaden the rift in the marriage, deepen the hurt, and increase the resistance inside our spouses. But if we look to God for instruction, he will show us how to use our words for healing rather than for hurt.

Each conversation with your spouse has the potential of steering things in a new direction. And it can change for the negative or positive, depending on how he perceives it. Whether or not you plan to, everything you do or say around your mate influences the course of your relationship. If you consciously choose your words and responses, the tone of your interaction—and perhaps your future—could be redirected. Even careful listening can send a message as you interpret your husband's words in a negative or positive way.

Allow God to minister to your heart. If it is pure and focused on him, your words will offer fresh manna to feed your hurting souls. Don't try to coerce your husband or shame him. Once you have expressed your anger in a calm and rational way, let God do the convicting. Pray for the wisdom to guard your lips. Then continue to pray that God will open your husband's eyes and heart.

> *Pleasant words are a honeycomb,*
> *sweet to the soul and healing to the bones.*
> —PROVERBS 16:24

A JOURNEY OF SUFFERING

> *My God, my God, why have You forsaken me?*
> *[Why are You] so far from my deliverance and*
> *from my words of groaning? My God, I cry by day,*
> *but You do not answer, by night, yet I have no rest.*
> —PSALM 22:1–2 HCSB

Although those words might have been spoken by you or me, they were actually the words of Israel's most famous king, David, as he was being pursued by the armies of Saul, who was trying to kill him before David attained the throne.

God had watched Saul turn from him in disobedience on a regular basis because of pride. God didn't want Israel's next king to stray as well, so he chose a different route for David. Instead of immediately going from shepherd boy to king, David went through years of trials and testing. His many lamentations in the Psalms show us the agony of his circumstances: "My God, I cry by day, but You do not answer" (Ps. 22:2 HCSB). By the time David became king, his heart of faith was strengthened. With a humble heart he was able to honor his faithful God throughout his reign.

David was just one of the noble people in the Bible who endured years of suffering before becoming the beloved hero of the faith we know today. Another was Moses, who was chosen before birth to be the deliverer of the Hebrews. He was saved from death as a baby and raised in the palace by the Pharaoh's daughter. But God gave him a humble life tending sheep as an alien in a foreign land for many years before using him to lead his people out of Egypt. As a young man, Moses lashed out in pride and anger to kill an Egyptian who abused a Hebrew slave. But many years later, after becoming the leader of his people, Moses is described as "a very humble man, more humble than anyone else on the face of the earth" (Num. 12:3).

Most heart-wrenching of all was Joseph. Although virtuous, honest, and faithful to God, he was betrayed by his brothers, sold into slavery, then condemned to prison for a crime he didn't commit. When we read about his dream as a young boy, we see that God knew about the famine and Joseph's high position in Egypt years later. God knew what would happen to take Joseph from being a boy in his father's land to a leader in Egypt. And the route was one of suffering. God knew, and God allowed it. Why? Joseph's own words to his brothers provide the answer: "You intended to harm me, but God intended it for good to accomplish what is now being done, the saving of many lives" (Gen. 50:20).

You are probably asking, like I used to, "Why is this happening to me? If God really loves me, why does he allow me to suffer?" God loved Moses, David, and Joseph, too, and yet he allowed them to suffer. Why? Because only through their suffering could they become the strong yet humble men of character who accomplished great things for their Lord. During their times of suffering each learned some of the deeper mysteries of God. They became pliable in his hands as they yielded to him in humility and learned to trust him with complete surrender of will. They became strong leaders who could endure the criticism of others and remain steadfast and patient during the silences and complexities of troubled times.

Maybe you don't aspire to become a great leader like David or Moses or Joseph, but hopefully you do aspire to become a woman of depth and character who can withstand the pressures of life in this world. Drought drives roots deeper into the ground so the plant can become stronger and withstand severe weather conditions. Suffering causes you to go deeper with God. As he takes you into a deeper life with him through your trials, you will find spiritual treasures that enrich your life and the lives of others. Allow God to carve out a place for himself in the midst of your suffering.

> Lord, I can't thank you for my suffering, but I can thank you for what you're going to do through my suffering. I know you are in control of all things. I know your plans are greater than mine. Help me stay strong through these difficult days so I can rejoice in the good things you will bring out of this.

A SPIRITUAL SACRIFICE

You also, like living stones, are being built into a spiritual house to be a holy priesthood, offering spiritual sacrifices acceptable to God through Jesus Christ.

—1 PETER 2:5

As I wound through a series of short streets connecting our neighborhood to one nearby, my eyes rested on a familiar house. I often traveled this route, and whenever I came around this curve and looked straight ahead, that house was always there. At that particular moment it gave me an odd sense of security to know I could depend on that house standing there every time I made that turn. I needed to know that some things stayed the same.

In my own life, there was nothing up ahead that my mind could hold onto. I was like a blind person traveling in a fog. The familiar structures were gone. Every step took me into uncharted territory.

I didn't know if this man who had been my husband for more than twenty years would ever be a part of my life again. We hadn't seen each other for four months. I knew he was more lost than I was. He had left his home, family, and friends, and he had strayed from God. I knew he felt defeated and confused.

Rounding one corner and then the next, I thought about how unpredictable all of life was—and how relatively short. "What is your life?" asks James 4:14. "You are a mist that appears for a little while and then vanishes."

I began praying. "God, I don't know if he will be my husband in this life anymore. But as my brother in Christ, help him to seek an intimate relationship with you. Even if I don't spend any more time with him on this earth, I want him to be right with you. If I can't love him as a husband, give me the ability to at least love him as my brother in Christ. And as my brother in Christ, bring him back into fellowship with you. After that we'll see what happens."

It was one of the hardest prayers I ever prayed.

It is hard to put your own pain to one side and pray for the person who is hurting you. Genuinely seeking God's love and interceding on behalf of a person who is turning your world upside down is like laying your heart on a railroad track and leaving it there while you board a train going off in the opposite direction. You are so vulnerable.

But in God's eyes, it is a spiritual sacrifice that enables him to turn the brokenness of your heart into soft clay that God can mold into something beautiful that he can use for an eternal purpose. God may need you to be a vessel through which he pours his grace into the needy, fragmented spaces of your husband's soul. You may be the priest God has chosen to stand in the gap for your husband's relationship with God. Your fervent prayers may be the vehicle through which the Holy Spirit moves to touch your husband and bring him to repentance and wholeness.

Are you willing to let God use the broken pieces of your heart as living stones to build his kingdom? Are you willing to give him your pain as a spiritual sacrifice so he can bless the lives of others, perhaps your husband? If you are not strong enough to set aside your pain in order to pray for him, ask God to give you the strength to do it. Eventually, as you allow God to pour his Holy Spirit into your pain, your heart will expand through his love, grace, and mercy until you are filled to overflowing. Then you may be able to experience the miracle of God's redeeming love as your prayers become a conduit between God and your husband, and you are initiated as a servant into God's holy priesthood.

> *Offer your bodies as living sacrifices, holy and pleasing to God—this is your spiritual act of worship.*
> —ROMANS 12:1

LIVING STONES

> *Pray continually; give thanks in all circumstances, for this is God's will for you in Christ Jesus.*
> —1 THESSALONIANS 5:17–18

*W*hen my husband and I first reconciled, I would run into people who had not seen us since the beginning of our crisis. I often saw the same question in their eyes: "How did you do it?"

If I had one word to answer them, it would, of course, be *God*. If I had two words, they would be *God* and *prayer*.

Prayer gave me the peace and strength to get through, and prayer was the power that brought changes to move my mountains. At times I saw prayers answered right before my eyes; at other times, I waited while answers seemed to hang suspended in the heavens.

During a time of estrangement, if a wife offers advice to her husband, he will likely identify that advice with her and become more resistant. But when she prays for him, God can convict him of the truth. God alone can reach into a husband's heart and bring about a change in his desires. When we stop striving to change another person and simply pray for him, we release him into God's hands. Then God is able to work more freely.

As I reached out to God in the middle of my circumstances, I prayed prayers of repentance about the part I had played in our marriage problems; I prayed prayers of thanksgiving for the blessings my dim eyes failed to recognize; I prayed prayers of petition when I sought God to perform miraculous changes in my husband and me for the restoration of our marriage; and I prayed prayers of spiritual warfare when I fought against the enemy of my husband's soul and mine.

But there were also prayers so hard to utter I had to dig down deep into a breaking heart to pull up the words; prayers that relinquished my husband into God's hands and asked for God to bless him whether or not we reconciled. Somehow I suspect it may have been those prayers, more than any others that touched God's heart of mercy.

First Peter 2:5 talks about us being living stones whose purpose is to offer up spiritual sacrifices to God. What is a living stone?

A living stone is strong, but not hard. It is solid and unshakable in the world, but alive and pliable to God. A living stone is a person who *abides* with Jesus. When Jesus says, "Bless those who curse you, pray for those who mistreat you" (Luke 6:28), he asks us to be *living stones*. In our situation we become living stones when we sacrificially offer up prayers on behalf of our husbands.

When we are able to set aside our pain in order to pray for our husbands, our hearts will connect to God to bring about a peace that genuinely surpasses understanding and a fullness of his presence that quenches our deep thirst for love. We become like the nozzle of a hose that connects to a faucet. As we give up our *right* to feel pain, we are giving up part of ourselves in order to connect to him. We enable him to pour his Spirit into us, filling us so we are more alive and complete than before. We become a conduit between God and humans, filled with enough grace to pour onto others.

As you focus on God, lift your voice to him in supplication. Let your requests be made known to him. Immerse yourself in prayer. God is near. Cry out to him. Just as we need to finish running a race before we can win the prize, we must continue on in this course before we can know the victory he has in store for us.

> God, fill me with your Spirit. Show me how to pray. Lord, I want to love as you love, but you know how hard it is for me right now. I need your strength to do what you want me to do. Soften my heart as you pour your healing balm into my pain.

SILVER AND GOLD

These [trials] have come so that your faith—
of greater worth than gold, which perishes
even though refined by fire—may be proved
genuine and may result in praise, glory and
honor when Jesus Christ is revealed.

—1 PETER 1:7

God loves us just the way we are, but he loves us too much to leave us there. He longs to draw out the beauty he sees within, but that beauty is frequently dimmed by the tarnish gathering on the surface of the soul. Impurities—from the world's influence and dross collected from childhood—settle among the rich nuggets of gold and silver within us that intermittently shine forth in precious moments of illumination. But their radiance is too quickly gobbled up in the shadows and futility of our own stubbornness and short-sightedness.

Although it is painful to suffer, God can use heartache—if we let him—to bring out the priceless treasure within us. These trials have come, says Peter, so that our "faith—of greater worth than gold, which perishes even though refined by fire—may be proved genuine and may result in praise, glory and honor when Jesus Christ is revealed" (1 Peter 1:7).

God wasn't surprised when this crisis occurred. He saw it coming, but for some reason he did not stop it, perhaps because he saw it as an opportunity to do greater things. First, he sees such things as an opportunity to draw us closer to him. We think God just wants us to be good and do things for him. But God's primary desire is for us to be in relationship with him. He longs for us to come and sit in his lap, talk to him, and read the Book he has given us. He is our Father. And he wants us to depend on him.

Secondly, he sees that a greater good than our own comfort can come out of our trials. He knows that if we learn to depend on him as a result of heartache and begin looking to him for direction, he can use these circumstances not only to bless us, but also to bless others. He has a plan, and it is a good plan. But we have to depend on him if we want to discover it.

James tells us to "consider it pure joy" whenever we face trials, because the testing of faith "develops perseverance," and "perseverance must finish its work so that [we] may be mature and complete" (1:2–3). At the beginning of the agonizing time of marital crisis, the suffering is too intense. The best we can do is just hang on to the hem of Jesus' garment and keep from being washed down a drainpipe in the middle of the flood of confusion and turmoil. But as this time of trial continues, and if our spiritual muscles become strong enough to keep us focused on God, he will begin to take us beyond the suffering into a new place. There he will develop our awareness of dark spots in our lives he wants to refine.

Often—and I know it was true of me—the sins that are the most menacing are also the most deceitful. They are so embedded within us that we can't see them. As we submit ourselves to the crucible of God's purposes, however, he purifies us and draws out the ugly stains of sin. But as long as we focus only on our pain and fight relentlessly for our rights, God cannot move us onto the next phase. It is natural to focus on our pain; it hurts; it cries out for attention. But after we allow God's healing balm to bind up the gaping wounds of our heart, we need to let God move us on to the restoration of our soul and the beauty for which he created us. He is the only one who can take our pain and pour it into the baptismal fire so it turns into a luster of gold.

In ancient times when gold was refined in fire, impurities would bubble to the surface. As workers skimmed these impurities off, they tested the results by looking into the metal. When they could see their image, they knew the gold was pure. God does the same with our lives. The Lord refines us continually throughout our time on earth, often using the trials we encounter along the way (see Mal. 3:3). When he finally sees his image within us, he knows he has attained his highest purpose for us. If we hold on to God and walk the path he has laid out for us during this difficult time, the integrity of our lives will turn into the luster of gold.

Lord, on my knees I look to you and call out your name, asking you to heal not only the pain in my heart, but the sin that darkens my soul. Let me humble myself in your presence and accept your ways. Let me surrender my willfulness to your majesty. Purify my life, O Lord. Cleanse my heart.

When he has tested me, I will come forth as gold.
                                             —JOB 23:10

WATER INTO WINE

When the wine was gone, Jesus' mother said to him,
"They have no more wine." ... [She] said to the ser-
vants, "Do whatever he tells you." ... Jesus said to
the servants, "Fill the jars with water"; so they filled
them to the brim. Then he told them, "Now draw
some out and take it to the master of the banquet."
They did so, and the master of the banquet tasted
the water that had been turned into wine.
                                       —JOHN 2:3, 5, 7–9

Sometimes the Lord asks us to do something that doesn't seem to make sense. It didn't make sense to the servants to fill the jars up with water when what they needed was wine. Can you imagine their trepidation at being asked to take water to the master of the wedding banquet? What would he think? Would he be annoyed? But they did it anyway. And not only did they end up with new wine to serve the guests, but the master was delighted, if not puzzled, that it was even better than the wine originally served (see John 2:10).

God's ways are not our ways. His purposes are beyond our own. He may ask us to do something that seems irrelevant, even contrary, to the crisis going on around us, but when we obey, we'll see his miracles and experience his blessings.

In the Old Testament another story provides an opposite picture. It is a portrait of *disobedience*—the story of Saul. God anointed Saul as king with the idea that Saul would have a kingdom for all time. But Saul's initial compliance quickly evaporated as he started substituting his judgment for God's. His willfulness surfaced most dramatically when he disobeyed the prophet Samuel's instructions.

Israel's enemies, the Philistines, had assembled to fight against Saul and his people. Samuel instructed Saul to wait seven days for his arrival so he could offer sacrifices to God before the battle. But on the seventh day, when Saul saw his troops growing fearful and beginning to scatter, he grew impatient and offered the burnt sacrifices himself. Of course, as soon as he finished, Samuel arrived and sternly rebuked him for his disobedience. Most important, Samuel withdrew God's blessing. "Now your kingdom will not endure; the LORD has sought out a man after his own heart and appointed him leader of his people, because you have not kept the LORD's command" (1 Sam. 13:14).

When I first read that story about Saul, I'd been separated from my husband for a year, and he was aloof and uncommunicative. I was restless, fearful, and anxious to have things all figured out. But when I read about Saul, I realized that I risked losing whatever blessings God might have planned for me. The story convicted me that I needed to wait on God for his timing and resist the urge to act prematurely.

God not only wants us to obey him in the easy things, he also wants our obedience when it's difficult, when it requires patience, when it means trusting that what he asks us to do is what he *really* wants us to do—even when it doesn't make sense. Saul's incredible blessing of a kingdom for all time was revoked because he could not wait on God just a little longer.

You may be in such a test right now. Fear may be a constant companion. You may have a hard time being patient and trusting God to work things out in your marriage. But if you act hastily and try to handle things yourself, you may miss out on the blessings God wants to give you. Don't try to tweak his commands to fit your own purposes. Resist trying to bend his Word to your own comfort level.

If we want to see God turn crisis into blessing and water into wine, if we want to see his life-changing miracles in our life, we must trust him enough to obey him with our whole heart. (For the complete story of Saul summarized above, read 1 Samuel 10:8; 13:1–14; 15:1–23.)

> God, give me the patience to wait on you. I don't want to miss out on the blessing you have in store for me. You know my pain. You know my anxiety. You know how easy it is for me to twist your words to suit my own purposes. I put my life in your hands. I will trust you. I choose to trust you. Give me the strength to wait in your embrace as you turn water into wine.

WITHOUT A ROAD MAP

I do remember writing this, I thought. *It seems like a thousand years ago now. Right before everything in our marriage fell apart.*

I looked at the answer I had checked in the *Experiencing God* (LifeWay, 1990) study guide as well as my comment. Then I reread the question. "Are you ready to follow God's will that way?"

The lesson told how Abram had followed God one day at a time. He didn't start out with a road map telling him all the details; he was just told to "go to the land I will show you" (Gen. 12:1). Abram obeyed without knowing where God would take him. I'd started the study three years earlier but had only gotten through the first three weeks.

I read the question again. "Are you ready to follow God's will that way?" My previous answer was still there. I had checked "other" and written, *I want to be able to do that.*

I could hear the rain softly falling in the street outside the open windows of our living room as I stared at the eight words I had written on the page three years before. *I want to be able to do that.* The words blurred, and my mind froze as images paraded before my mind, emerging from the dark cloud of memory I was eager to put behind me. For a moment I was standing in the light at the end of a dark tunnel, looking back into the bleak depths from where I had recently emerged. I saw my husband and me doing this lesson three years before.

We were sitting in the living room. Slumped in the burgundy chair, my husband read a question flippantly, "What does God want you to do in response to today's study? Nothing," he said.

"Nothing? What do you mean nothing?" I asked hesitantly.

"God has already done it, and I don't have to do anything. Right? So God wants me to do nothing."

I looked at him questioningly, trying to rationalize away the apathy of his answer, hoping he was just being funny. He had been so hard to understand over the past two years. "That's all?" I asked.

"Am I supposed to answer honestly the way I see it or am I supposed to answer the way I think you want me to answer it?"

"Honestly, of course."

"Well, then, 'Nothing.'"

Shadows continued rising from the tunnel of my mind as glimpses of the days following this exchange flickered through my memory: the dining-room table sparkling with our best china and silver, the Easter ham baking in the oven, my mother and I talking at the kitchen table. Then yelling ...

Instead of celebration, the anger that had been simmering in my husband for the past two years erupted as years of suppressed feelings were unleashed. I lashed back angrily, matching his assault, our verbal darts zeroing in on their respective targets. Then he left.

Hours passed and he didn't return. My mother went home. Our daughters wandered around the house not knowing what to say. Numbly I stared at the dining-room table, too dazed to put the dishes back in the cupboard or remove the decorations. *Surely he'll come back tomorrow.* But he didn't.

The image of the table lingered in my mind as I remembered how it stood mocking me during the next few days, still unspoiled, ready for celebration—as the darkness of a crumbling marriage fell upon our home.

Those first turbulent days stretched into weeks, then months, with every day standing still in a lost moment of time, barely creeping forward. The pain, the loneliness, the anxiety. I languished with the helpless feeling that my world had disintegrated before my eyes. Would the agony never end?

Gradually, the heartache led to questions, and I began to search the past for answers. We had been so deeply in love when we got married. We called ourselves halves. But our blurred senses of identity caused unrealistic expectations of one another. Instead of halves, I realized we had regarded each other more like appendages. Each of us expected the other to think and feel as we did. We didn't, and we weren't able to bridge the gap of that misunderstanding. Gradually, we forged a trail of poor communication, which finally led to an impasse.

I was from an assertive family where honestly expressed feelings were the norm. He had an upbringing where harmony was more important than openness. To him conflict was to be avoided. To me conflict was to be brought out into the open and resolved. Over time I became resentful of the unresolved problems that persisted in our marriage, and he began to feel threatened by my assertiveness. To escape his disappointments, he began living a separate life. I became bitter and sarcastic about his lack of participation in the home. He became angry, and, to me, appeared irrational. One layer formed upon another until it was difficult to see what the root problem was. I didn't know how we could ever cut through the layers to find a resolution. It seemed hopeless.

The dripping of the rain outside brought me back to the present. I looked again at the words I had once written in ink on the page before me, "I want to be able to do that."

The possible responses were:

- No, I don't think God will ever ask me to go any-where that he doesn't show me ahead of time where I am going.
- I'm not sure.
- Yes, I am willing to follow him by faith and not by sight.
- Other.

My eyes rested on the third choice. "Yes, I am willing," it read. My head fell back against the sofa. I closed my eyes. *Was I willing?*

I remembered hearing God's voice as I'd heard it in the car that morning a year and a half after my husband had left. "I'm going to make a new person of you," God seemed to say.

I'd been praying, crying out to God, "How long? How long are we going to be separated? Why is it taking so long?"

And that is when I had heard those inaudible but distinct words. "I'm going to make a new person of you—and it takes a long time to do that."

Yes, it had been a long time. My mind rested on images, words, specific passages of encouragement from the Bible. For 1,095 days I had taken one step at a time with nothing to hold on to, nothing to believe in—except the Lord.

But God accomplished his purpose. He indeed melted and molded me into a new person. And not just me but Marv as well. I remembered the week I went on a modified fast. At the end of the week, my heart was soft and supple and sensitive to God's voice.

In the following weeks and months, Marv and I formed a cautious friendship, not with any depth, but with a light touch—going to movies and having fun. I remembered the next Christmas, almost a year later, when we were joking around about some gifts in a Christmas exchange at his office party. Suddenly he grabbed me and kissed me. I sank into his arms and cried. The joy of his closeness mingled painfully with the distance time had carved between us. I thought I'd never feel the touch of his lips on mine again.

From that point we tiptoed into the fearful and uncertain challenges of honesty and restoration. Our counselor told us to invite one another into the closets of secrecy that each of us guarded so we could allow our hearts to connect once again. We went on a Retrouvaille weekend for troubled marriages. Through the communication tools Retrouvaille offered, my husband was, for the first time, able to identify and express how he felt about certain issues that were important to him and our marriage. On my part, I was able to feel understood. Finally, we'd dug beneath the rubbish and once again discovered our hearts of love. We had the beginning back.

I looked down again at the question and answer in my workbook:

> "Are you ready to follow God's will that way?"
> "I want to be able to do that."

My eyes brightened as the realization hit me. "And I did!" I said aloud. *Thank you, Lord. I did follow you without knowing where you'd take me. And now here I am. Slowly, one day at a time, you changed me and you changed him and you brought us back together.*

I heard a rustling and looked up. Marv moved to the burgundy chair and sat down with his own study book. "Hi," I said, pushing the cobwebs out of my mind.

He smiled. "After you get through the week of studies, we can go through them together."

"Are you finished with your study?" I asked.

"Yes," he said. "I'm just using the same book as last time."

"Oh? So you're writing new responses? Or using the old ones?"

"I'm writing new ones." He paused in awkward reflection. "I'm finding my old answers seem kind of shallow."

"Hmmm," I said. "It's always interesting to compare your responses like that. You can see what God has done in your life between then and now."

My answer seemed so soft in my ears. There was no, "Well, of course! What would you expect?" My curt responses had been all too frequent.

"Well, I think I'm going to bed," he said, getting up from the chair. He walked over and kissed me good night.

I watched him go, then looked back down at the choices on the page before me, particularly the third one. "Yes, I am willing to follow him by faith and not by sight." I checked the box.

Now I could say that without hesitating. God had clearly taken me through the past three years one step at a time. I hadn't had a road map, only the Lord. And we made it. How many times had I fought the urge to utter a sarcastic comment or a word of rebuke? How many hours had I lain draped over the bed in prayer, struggling to focus on God instead of giving into peevish attitudes? *Lord, if I had done it my way, we wouldn't be where we are.*

Yes, one day at a time, God had changed me into a new person, and because of that I had been able to put my husband and my marriage in the Lord's hands. I had followed God by faith and not by sight. It had been a long road. But we made it.

Part 4

HEART CONNECTIONS: WALKING THROUGH THE SHARDS

My God will meet all your needs according to his glorious riches in Christ Jesus.

—PHILIPPIANS 4:19

IF NO ONE SEES

*Look at the birds of the air; they do not sow or
reap or store away in barns, and yet your heavenly Father feeds them. Are you not much more
valuable than they?*

—MATTHEW 6:26

S itting on the dock of a lake one late afternoon, I was cap-
tivated by the sight of an exquisite sunset. The colors
melting into one another to illuminate the sky stirred the
lonely places of my heart. Although clouds had enveloped my
soul moments before, I found myself praising God, thanking
him for this beautiful sunset and the opportunity to see it.

I felt the Spirit of God asking me, "But what if you didn't
see it? Would the sunset still be as beautiful?"

"Yes," I said, "it would still be just as beautiful."

"And what if *no one* saw this sunset, would it still be just as
beautiful?"

"Yes, it would still be just as beautiful."

"And if I make a person beautiful, but no one loves her, is
she still beautiful?" God's Spirit inquired.

"Yes," I said, "she would still be beautiful."

"I made you beautiful ... and I love you. So if your husband
does not see your beauty, does that mean you are not beautiful?
If he does not love you, does that mean you are not loved?"

"No," I whispered. "I do not need anyone else to love me or
think I am beautiful. You are enough, Lord. If you love me and
think I am beautiful, then that is enough."

"I loved you enough to die for you," he said. "I created
you to be the unique person that you are. You are beautiful. I
love you."

At that I bowed my head in praise and worshipped him in
love.

I praise you, Lord, for you are wonderful.
Thank you for seeing me through eyes of
love. Thank you for making me your special
child.

Sweet Dependence

Suspended between heaven and earth, I wait.

The earth, which seemed secure, now trembles.
Tenderly,
God's unseen hand
holds me above the dust of broken dreams.

Longingly,
I grope through crumbling remains of gold rings
and promises of love, searching
for gems of hope.

But wrapped in God's gentle cloak of love,
the memory of bitter clashes,
dark eyes and angry words
stays my rush to resolution
lest my love's return should turn to sand beneath
      my feet
where familiar landscapes and jagged artifacts
threaten to sever the cord of sweet dependence
that, in loving suspension,
holds me as I wait.

HANGING ON

Cast your cares on the LORD and he will sustain
you; he will never let the righteous fall.

—PSALM 55:22

*I*n the picture on the wall, my daughter Julie stands on the pinnacle of a mountain, gazing out over the scenic valley at the foot of the rocky cliffs she has just scaled. She holds the pose of the conqueror, the victor, the rock climber who has met the challenge and surmounted the obstacles.

But, as with all of us, before becoming the victor, she first had to face the challenge.

As a college student Julie was drawn to rock climbing. Linked together by a rope, she and her friends would scale the side of a mountain, inching their way upward, grabbing hold of outcroppings. Finding these outcroppings became their greatest challenge, for occasionally there was nothing substantial ahead of them to reach for. Instead, they would be forced to grasp for whatever shallow hold they could find with mere fingertips.

Julie told me about a time when she was hanging, her full weight supported by a tiny jutting of rock, her fingers burning, her strength waning. Scanning the rocks above her, she searched for another outcropping that was more secure, but the rapid loss of strength immediately sapped her of the will to continue. She wanted to give up and go back. But she couldn't. Although she was afraid to let go of the fragile hold for fear she would fall, she knew in actuality that the only way to *keep* from falling was to let go and continue upward.

Fastening her eyes on the goal above her, she mustered all her determination, then let go. For one brief moment, the peril of her plight gripped her with fear. She was certain she was falling. But with a strength she didn't know she possessed, she forced herself to reach for another hold. As her fingers touched the security of a higher rock, she experienced the exhilaration of relief. She could rest and renew her strength. She felt secure.

With a new perspective she looked down at the arduous slope she had just climbed. It was doable. She had gotten through it. Even though it had seemed impossible at the time, she succeeded through the power of her will and the determination to move on to her goal. And despite her fears, she knew down deep that even in her peril she was safe because the rope around her waist was securely fastened at the top of the mountain.

In the pain and precariousness of your crises, you may feel as though you, too, are scaling the side of a mountain where there is nothing to hold onto. You can't see to the top and don't know what is up there even if you should make it. It is too hard, and you're ready to give up.

At these times God's strength is sufficient, and he freely gives it to all who ask. You only need enough strength to take the next step, to reach for the next promise of his word and take hold of the Rock. "'Not by might nor by power, but by my Spirit,' says the Lord Almighty" (Zech. 4:6).

"If the Lord delights in a man's way, he makes his steps firm; though he stumble, he will not fall, for the Lord upholds him with his hand" (Ps. 37:23–24). Whenever you feel as though you are going to fall, remember the true security of the rock climber. Even were she to slip, she is sustained by a rope that holds her to the other climbers and to a secure abutment at the top of the mountain. You, too, are held by God's invisible cord of love and grace. It will not fail you. As long as you are reaching out to him, he will be the rock of your salvation. He will not let you fall.

Father, sustain me and I will live; don't let my hopes be dashed. I kneel before you, Father, from whom your whole family in heaven and on earth derives its name. I pray that out of your glorious riches you will strengthen me with power through your Spirit in my inner being, so that

Christ may dwell in my heart through faith. Let me hold unswervingly to the hope I profess, for I know that you who promised will be faithful. You alone are my Rock and my salvation; you are my fortress, I will never be shaken.
—PRAYER ADAPTED FROM PSALM 119:116; EPHESIANS 3:14–17; HEBREWS 10:23; PSALM 62:2.

WEAPONS

The weapons we fight with are not the weapons of the world. On the contrary, they have divine power to demolish strongholds.
—2 CORINTHIANS 10:4

Our minds are wondrous things. We learn to analyze situations and decide on the best course of action. We find creative solutions. We remember past behaviors that worked and apply them to new experiences. We learn to use certain words to get what we want in life and induce others to respond according to our wishes. Sometimes we accomplish our goals through our actions. We make ourselves look more attractive, prepare a nice dinner, do someone a favor, or buy a gift. We may withhold pleasure from our children or our mate to teach them a lesson, or even use negative behavior to prompt a desired response.

These are weapons of this world. We spend much of our lives using such tactics to accomplish our purposes. We have a good idea what we want, and we figure it is up to us to get it to work out that way.

But when we are in crisis, life doesn't seem to be playing by the same rules anymore. Normal patterns are not working. The weapons of this world are no longer worthy of the battle. It's as though we are shooting with bows and arrows when we need to be firing a missile.

To find the proper weapons for the battle you are in, turn to God. They are not what you normally think of as weapons— not a good tongue-lashing, not the cold shoulder, not an attempt to make him jealous, not throwing his clothes out on the street. No, God's weapons will often surprise us, but they come with his mighty power, and they alone can demolish strongholds.

Making full use of God's weapons, however, first requires a full surrender to him. He is not only our ally, but our commander. He gives us the weapons, but he also tells us how to fight the battle, what front to fight on, and in what order. Sometimes, as in the battle of Jericho, he tells us not to storm the gates, but to walk around outside the walls several times.

Or he may have us work on our armor first. You see, God is sovereign. He knows when our armor has a weakness in it, and he knows how to mend it so we don't receive a fatal blow. That might be his first priority.

One of his greatest weapons is prayer. He will want to teach us how to pray because prayer can indeed demolish strongholds.

Are you prepared to enlist yourself in God's army, recognize him as your commander, and fight the battle his way? Are you willing to let him train you for effective spiritual warfare?

> *Put on the full armor of God so that you can take your stand against the devil's schemes.*
> —Ephesians 6:11

HOW MUCH TO SAY TO WHOM

Set a guard over my mouth, O LORD;
keep watch over the door of my lips.

—PSALM 141:3

s I felt my brother's strong arms encircle me, I buried my face into his shoulder and sobbed, my chest heaving in and out within his firm embrace. Neither of us could believe what I was telling him—that my husband had left me.

Over the next few days as we talked, I could tell that he was suffering with me. He admitted crying out to God on my behalf and shedding tears, a rare show of emotion. But they were precious moments for me in the midst of that awful time. My brother, in his love for me, allowed himself to feel the depth of my private pain. The knowledge of his love carried me through many difficult times.

But it was not my brother with whom I shared the deepest bitterness of my soul.

Despite his love—or perhaps because of it—I sensed that sharing my bitterness with him could leave a lasting scar that might be harder to erase than my own. I wanted to leave the door open to the future—a future that I hoped would include my husband as well as my brother. I knew it would be hard enough for me to forgive; I didn't want to lay that burden on him as well.

Guarding future relationships should be considered whenever you choose to share your deepest feelings with someone. You may first want to evaluate each person's ability to forgive and forget. Unloading the bitterness of your heart on family and close friends could cause collateral damage and multiply the wounds that need to be healed should you reconcile. But you need to unload that bitterness somewhere. It may be family, but it may not. And if not, where? How do we decide?

Whom to Trust

At this vulnerable point in your life, your primary concern needs to be how a confidant's reactions, advice, and responses will affect your heart. Does the person have wisdom? Does she share your principles? Can she offer God's perspective?

My counselor speaks of counseling as an important component, not "so that a person can be instructed and given advice. It's more of a safe place to be honest, a safe place for the hidden purposes of the heart, like in Proverbs 20:5, which says, 'the purposes of a man's heart are deep waters, but a man of understanding draws them out.' In a separation (or severe marriage crisis) there are all kinds of undercurrents going on." It is good to have someone wise enough to steer you in the right direction.

His comments are a good guide in deciding whom to talk to. Your goal is to find a safe place—a safe person—with whom to share the purposes of your heart. But it is also important whom we get our hope from. Is it from someone who says, "I got a divorce and I'm fine. You'll be fine too"? Or does hope come from people who believe in reconciliation—not to push it, but to support you with prayer, hope, and a word of encouragement when you ask for it?

As we travel this road, we need to weigh the advantages and disadvantages of sharing too much of our situation with various people, and then avoid indiscriminate and casual sharing of our deepest hurts with just anyone who will listen. Proverbs 20:19 warns, "A gossip betrays a confidence; so avoid a man who talks too much." How much do we want people to know about our problems should we be able to restore our marriage?

Not only should you think about your own needs, but also those of the people you share with. How will the unloading of your feelings affect them? Are they vulnerable themselves so that hearing about your circumstances might throw them into wrong thinking patterns?

Your children can be deeply affected by your words. They should be able to love and respect both parents at the other end of this crisis. To vindicate yourself to them, you may hurt them in many ways you do not intend. First Timothy 6:20 tells us to "guard what has been entrusted to your care. Turn away from godless chatter." Children are a gift from God, and we have a duty to shield them as much as possible from our words of anger and hurt during this time.

You need friends for this difficult journey. The right friend will be a port in the storm, someone who supports you, listens, and offers words of encouragement while challenging you to higher thoughts. But you need to thoughtfully consider how much to say to each person you encounter along the way.

> Lord, I need friends. I feel so alone. Please give me the discernment to know who to talk to, who will listen to me, and who will accept me just as I am in all my brokenness. Lead me to friends who will offer hope, encouragement, and words of wisdom.

He who guards his lips guards his life,
but he who speaks rashly will come to ruin.
—Proverbs 13:3

Discouraging Words and Encouraging People

The tongue that brings healing is a tree of life.
—Proverbs 15:4

Amanda was separated from her husband. Her heart was broken. Discouragement immobilized her to the extent that she was barely able to function. At lunch one day she looked at her friend across the table. "I can't even pray any more," she said.

Her friend nodded. "You know what, Amanda? That is okay. You don't have to pray right now. That's what your friends are for, and this is our time to carry you in our prayers."

Friends are one of the most important lifelines you have right now. Job's friends, in spite of their deficiencies, at least "showed up." And at first they offered consolation to Job by just sitting beside him in his grief. It was when they began to speak and question the integrity of his character that they lost credibility. For in the end, they just added to his pain.

Often our friends are just the opposite. They don't accuse; instead they want to make us feel good. They do this by justifying us in our decisions and responses, volunteering advice based on their own experiences, or offering empty platitudes. Sometimes in doing this they unintentionally support us in ways that lead us along the road to divorce. They can't imagine the possibility of our marriage being restored. Such was the danger Brenda encountered with her neighbor Tanya.

Tanya leaned back in the chair and took a sip of wine. "I've never known a man who had John's problem to be able to change." She looked knowingly at Brenda, who had recently become aware of some dysfunctional behaviors in her husband. "My ex had the same problem." She shook her head. "They never change."

Brenda shivered as pinpricks nettled through her heart. Her eyes opened wide in alarm. "I don't want a divorce," Brenda said. "I just want him to realize what he's doing."

Tanya shook her head again. "He's got all the signs. He won't change."

That night in bed Brenda tossed and turned. Was she being naïve? Was Tanya right? Was it impossible for John to change? Her heart felt like lead. The skin on her forehead felt stretched and tight as her mind raced. She didn't want her marriage to end.

Brenda knew God had led her this far in making her aware of the problem and enabling her to confront John in the first place. She would listen to God the rest of the way too. But first she needed to quiet the voices that threatened to steer her off course. She determined not to discuss her marriage with her neighbor again.

Discouragement is easy to find in our present crisis. At the grocery store we run into a friend who has heard about our separation, and before long she is telling us about mutual friends who've recently gotten divorced. We see a divorced friend at the mall who begins to tell us her war stories, which are "like ours." Other friends say nothing, or worse, they seem to avoid us. They don't know what to say or do. They want to spare us the discomfort of their own awkwardness.

Then there's the kind of friend we all need who comes up to us at church. Her voice is warm and caring. Her eyes reach out to us to draw us into the warm circle of her concern. "I heard what happened," she says. "How are you doing?" She doesn't push or probe, but she invites us to call, to get together and talk if we want. For me, this was Kathy, who helped me stay connected, to be encouraged, and eventually make it to the other side.

Friends who encourage and challenge us to better things are invaluable. But if they had a similar experience to ours that turned out badly, we may need to keep in mind that a tinge of their own bitterness may pepper their words of advice and counsel. Proverbs 17:22 says, "A cheerful heart is good medicine, but a crushed spirit dries up the bones." If you are sharing with a friend, and her response causes your heart to sink with feelings of hopelessness about your marriage, chances are she is not the one to encourage you.

Seek out positive friends who hold you up in loving and prayerful support, ones who believe in reconciliation but don't force it. A wise friend will allow you to pour out your heart and listen before jumping to conclusions and offering advice. And when she does make suggestions, her words will encourage, inspire, challenge, and comfort.

Discouraging comments, however, will come regardless of how much you try to guard against them. When a discouraging word sears your heart, take it to God and lay it at his feet. Of all your friends, he will always be the most faithful and wise.

Dear Lord, encourage my heart. Give me hope. Bring me friends to help me hold myself together.

*A word aptly spoken is like
apples of gold in settings of silver.*
—PROVERBS 25:11

CHILDREN CAUGHT IN THE PAIN

*Each of you should look not only to your own
interests, but also to the interests of others.*
—PHILIPPIANS 2:4

After my husband and I first reconciled, my daughter Laura walked in the door one day, her eyes dancing. "I heard a new song on the radio by Shania Twain. It should be Daddy's and your song! It's called 'You're Still the One.'"

A warm glow spread through me. Laura was right. The agonizing nights were over. The fears, the doubts were behind me. But as I looked into her smiling eyes, I remembered that this story wasn't just about my husband and me. The story of our daughters and the impact all of this had on them was there too. Their lives and hearts were affected just as ours were. But because of their youth, they often didn't know how it was affecting them or how to respond to it.

When we are buried in our own grief, it's hard to see the pain of our children. We think of ourselves as the victims and our children as mere bystanders—observers. But they are victims too. What they thought was rock has turned to sand. The safety net that should protect them and give them security has sprung a gaping hole.

As we reel within a world that is turning upside down, so do they. Whether they are toddlers or young adults, our children walk along behind us, the dust we kick up flying in their faces, the garbage of our words becoming sour food in their minds, our silences and insensitivities spinning a web of confusion and disconnectedness over their souls. Sometimes their confused emotions cause them to drift into actions that alarm us. They may pull away in rebellion or sink into depression or isolation. These are the innocents we love with every fiber of our being. How do we keep from hurting them?

First and most important, seek God to make sure *you* are going in the direction he would lead. You need to stay in his will. And each day, pray a hedge of protection around your children.

It is hard to comprehend the vulnerability children feel, which causes them to think your marriage problems are their fault. It is important to continually reassure them that this crisis is not their fault. Reinforce this to them throughout the turmoil—because they may not hear it or believe it the first time you say it.

In this out-of-control setting, keep life as normal as possible to preserve the children's sense of security. Be available, listen to them, and let them express their own upset feelings without judging them. This will give them the freedom to deal with their grief more honestly. Since you may not be able to listen to their pain without being distracted by your own, give them the freedom to share with friends. It may seem awkward, but remember that this is their crisis too.

You also need to keep them in the loop, letting them know the general scope of what is going on without sharing details they don't need to know. Resist the temptation to demonize their father or disparage or minimize their father's love for them. They need his love just as they need yours.

Your own intense anguish needs to be expressed in healthy forums. This is an opportunity for them to see God's supernatural power at work in you as you meet each day. If they see you looking to God and finding healthy outlets, such as friends or counselors, during this time of distress, your present pain can eventually bear fruit in your children's lives in years to come.

But in the midst of it all, you also need to give yourself a lot of grace—forgiving yourself for failures and asking your children for forgiveness as well. You cannot—and will not—be perfect. Pray with them for wisdom, strength, mercy, and understanding. They have their own path to walk, and as they navigate around the shards of their mom and dad's broken relationship, they too can use this part of the journey to learn and grow. You can diminish their pain by giving God center stage and letting him lead in his way and on his schedule.

> Lord, protect my children. Place a hedge around them and keep them in the circle of your love. It's so hard for me to see their pain when I am in the midst of mine. Give me the wisdom and sensitivity to listen and affirm them and steer them around the potholes in the road.

TEMPTATION

Have mercy on me, O God, according to your unfailing love; according to your great compassion blot out my transgressions. Wash away all my iniquity and cleanse me from my sin.

—PSALM 51:1–2

Victoria looked up from her desk, waiting for her boss's familiar smile, hoping he would take the time to stop and chat a minute as he often did. Instead he stopped at the desk of her co-worker and patiently showed her some mistakes in a report he wanted her to correct. Victoria felt her heart beating faster as she watched him. She loved his confidence, his gentle authority.

Why couldn't Kevin be like that? Why was her husband making her take all the responsibility for their finances—as well as taking care of the kids and the cooking and the cleaning? She sighed and pictured him slouching around the house, sitting in front of the TV or on the patio smoking a cigarette instead of looking for a new job. *Why couldn't he pull himself together? Yes, he'd lost his job, but it wasn't the end of the world. There were other jobs out there.*

Her boss turned and took a step toward her. She caught his eye and swallowed hard. It wasn't that he was so good looking. He was actually rather tall and gangly. The fact that he was a strong Christian and would never entertain romantic thoughts of her made him even more attractive. He was the kind of man she wanted her husband to be.

When unresolved and prolonged troubles brew between you and your husband, you may feel tempted to look at other men with less restraint than before. Feeling rejected, misunderstood, or mistreated by your spouse may make you vulnerable to the advances of others, or, like Victoria, entice you to flirt with the idea of another man.

During a marriage crisis, temptation can lurk in the commonest places. But the Scripture is clear. Jesus says in Matthew 5:28, "Anyone who looks at a woman [or man] lustfully has already committed adultery with her [or him] in his [or her] heart." "Marriage should be honored by all, and the marriage bed kept pure, for God will judge the adulterer and all the sexually immoral" (Heb. 13:4). "You shall not covet your neighbor's wife [or husband]" (Ex. 20:17).

Even if you are separated, you are still married, and your marriage vows still apply. Willard Harley, author of *His Needs, Her Needs*, says it very clearly: "You are married until you are divorced. Separation is a state of marriage." Being separated does not free you to go on a date.

It is when we are the weakest that Satan tries to attack. When he sees a chink in our marriage, he will try to bring a bulldozer through. We need to guard our heart against these attacks, whether it is the temptation to enter into a sexual affair or a subtler affair of the heart. Nurturing quiet longings for another man may seem harmless at first, but an affair of the heart puts forth barbs that can drag us out of God's presence into a place of sin.

Sheep never plan to get lost. They graze and nibble their way off in the wrong direction, and before they know it, they have strayed from the shepherd into unknown territory. In the same way you can drift into relationships that lead you away from God. Sin can begin in the subtle guise of innocence but grow into something lethal.

Victoria was fortunate to have a wise Christian friend with whom she could share her dark secret, and her friend put a name to it—an affair of the heart. Despite Victoria's protests, her friend challenged her with the notion that she was enjoying her silent affair and didn't really want to give it up. Finally, realizing her attraction was merely an escape from the stress at home, Victoria went to the Lord with her friend and confessed it as sin.

The Bible encourages us in 1 Corinthians 10:13, "No temptation has seized you except what is common to man. And God is faithful; he will not let you be tempted beyond what you can bear. But when you are tempted, he will also provide a way out so that you can stand up under it." Through her friend, Victoria found the way out God had provided for her to resist Satan's snare, and eventually her husband pulled out from his depression, got a job, and together they reestablished a solid and fulfilling marriage.

If you find yourself tempted, look for the way out God has provided. Instead of harboring secret attractions, seek godly counsel. If you have not encountered this kind of temptation, continue guarding your heart against Satan's attack.

Relationships that develop from a needy emotional state usually turn out to be Band-Aid relationships. They temporarily cover up your pain, but eventually you will be looking for a waste can in which to discard it. One needy person latching onto another does not produce long-lasting, solid results.

Lord, guard my heart. Protect me from Satan's arrows and the lust of the eyes and flesh. Strengthen my resolve to do what is right in your eyes.

Do not conform ... to the pattern of this world,
but be transformed by the renewing of your mind.
—ROMANS 12:2

We are more than conquerors through him who
loved us.
—ROMANS 8:37

HIS STRENGTH IN OUR WEAKNESS

Humble yourselves, therefore, under God's mighty
hand, that he may lift you up in due time.
—1 PETER 5:6

J really had to struggle with self-righteousness," Penny said to me one day. Her world had been turned upside down when her husband, Nick, was arrested with a prostitute. She leaned forward on the sofa. "For his own personal spiritual restoration, Nick was focusing on Ephesians 2:8–9, which says, 'For it is by grace you have been saved, through faith—and this not from yourselves, it is the gift of God—not by works, so that no one can boast.' I realized that applied to me also."

She paused.

"It is not my works. I can't boast. It is grace. It is God's working through me that gives me the power to forgive Nick and to do anything. I come to the table with nothing. And that helped me deal with the temptation to be self-righteous."

When we look for change in our marriage, our mate, or ourselves, where does the power to make it happen come from? Change often seems impossible, or at best improbable. On one hand, we don't think we have the power to change anything significant, and we don't. On the other hand, we are responsible for our own actions. And that is where we fail.

When Penny and Nick were recovering from their marital crisis, their healing was marked by humility. Despite the sin Nick committed against her, Penny listened to the advice of her pastor and a trusted Christian friend. She submitted her will to God and examined herself to weed out and resist the sins of pride, self-righteousness, and slander. Although anger still simmered within her, she allowed eyes of compassion and a heart of humility and forgiveness to guide her.

On Nick's part, he submitted himself to the counsel of his pastor, and instead of being defensive, he welcomed reproach with an attitude of humility, openness, and honesty. He willingly became accountable to other Christians and to his wife.

By humbling themselves before God, Penny and Nick allowed God's power to work in and through their lives. Not only was their marriage completely healed and restored, but Penny's heart of forgiveness also witnessed to her father. Before he died two years later, the family realized he had been touched so deeply by the witness of Penny's humble and forgiving spirit that it opened the doors to a new spiritual receptiveness in him. He received Christ. And heaven opened its doors.

The power for change comes through our humility before God and one another. We cannot make it happen. Only God can. "[His] power is made perfect in [our] weakness" (2 Cor. 12:9). When we humble ourselves before God and relinquish the desire to be in control, we unleash his mighty power into our marriages to affect the changes we long for.

> Lord, I surrender all my self-righteousness, my pride, my desire to be in control. I give it all to you, Lord. I want my desires to conform to yours. Open the doors of my mind to your will. Loosen the tight places of my heart.

> *I pray also that the eyes of your heart may be enlightened in order that you may know ... his incomparably great power for us who believe. That power is like the working of his mighty strength, which he exerted in Christ when he raised him from the dead.*
> —EPHESIANS 1:18–20

IF

If we're off balance, He can hold us up.
If there's little we can say, He can speak.
If we can't see straight, He can lead.
If we have nothing, He can be everything.
If logic doesn't work, faith can.

THE UNSEEN BATTLE

For our struggle is not against flesh and blood,
but against the rulers, against the authorities,
against the powers of this dark world and against
the spiritual forces of evil in the heavenly realms.

—EPHESIANS 6:12

I'm so angry at him I don't even want to pray for him," Diane said. Her brow was furrowed, her eyes flashed in anger as she spoke to me.

Over our two-hour lunch, she described her husband as a kind, compassionate, and generous friend to everyone in the church while at home he was angry and demanding. She couldn't wait for him to walk out the door each morning to go to work. Their intimate home life was the best-kept secret in a church that saw him as a respected Christian leader and her as the perfect example of a submissive wife. But inside the walls of their home, Diane watched the man everyone else knew evaporate. She found him jealous, suspicious, and overbearing. She felt as though she constantly walked on eggshells around him.

I could see that in her mind, her bags were already packed. She was leaving. She had even thumbed through the classifieds looking for apartments to rent. She'd read every book and tried everything she could think of to please her husband and keep him from being so angry. Nothing worked.

"But I think that praying is exactly what you need to do," I said, thinking back to some red flags that had popped up in her story that sounded more like spiritual issues than character flaws or plain old sin.

"But I have prayed," she said. "I've tried everything. I'm over that."

"You may need gutsier prayers—spiritual warfare prayers. Sometimes regular prayers aren't enough."

"Really?"

"During the darkest days of our separation, I would do spiritual warfare on behalf of my husband three or four times a day."

"You're kidding."

"Satan doesn't want you to pray for your husband, because he knows your prayers have the power to break down the strongholds that are keeping him and your marriage in bondage."

"But he needs to want to make changes. I can't do it for him."

"Some of the things you've described sound like they have a deeper spiritual dimension to them rather than just being normal character flaws. Satan looks for our weaknesses, and that is where he attacks. Walt is a leader in the church. Satan would love to bring him and your marriage down. It would be a great victory for him."

After this discussion Diane and I agreed to join together in spiritual warfare prayer for her husband during the coming weeks. Within a couple of months the bitterness between them began to melt. She saw a difference between the times we were praying for him and the times we weren't. He became more open to discussion. And although there continued to be bumps along the road, their marriage began to heal.

When your spouse wrongs you and your anger rises up against him, praying for him may be the last thing you feel like doing. But that is one of Satan's deceptions. He uses *feelings* and *anger* to help justify you in relinquishing your husband to the darkness of Satan's snare. If your husband is entangled in sin, you cannot rescue him. Your words will not convince him. But God can. And you can be the instrument to unleash God's mighty power and squash Satan's hold on the man you are united to in marriage.

A stronghold in a person's life gives Satan access, and although as Christians we have been delivered from the *power* of darkness, we are not necessarily free from the *presence* of darkness. Too often we are ignorant of the disruptive role Satan is playing in the havoc around us. If we ignore him, we give him free rein.

When you take authority over the enemy in Jesus' name, you can loosen Satan's hold on your husband, your marriage, and yourself. But it takes active spiritual warfare prayer to defeat him. Satan's favorite tool is deception. He throws all kinds of lies to see which one sticks. But as Christians, we have been given the power to counteract the lies and half-truths of Satan with the truth of God.

Your husband is not your enemy. Satan is. Unleash your anger at Satan, and you may see the strongholds begin to dissolve.

> God, reveal to me any strongholds in my husband's life that I need to pray against. Open my eyes to the spiritual battle that might be going on in his life. Help me see with spiritual eyes so I can be an instrument for your divine purposes.

Be self-controlled and alert. Your enemy the devil prowls around like a roaring lion looking for someone to devour.

—1 Peter 5:8

A Practical Guide to Spiritual Warfare

From an Interview with Pastor Carl Stephens, Faith Assembly of God, Orlando, Florida

Why a Wife Should Pray Spiritual Warfare over Her Husband

"I believe that a wife's prayers for her husband are stronger than anyone else's prayers for him. When a wife prays for her husband or a husband prays for his wife, there is a dimension in the spirit realm that gives these prayers a greater spiritual force simply because of the fact that they are one. But usually the wife doesn't realize how powerful her prayers are.

"If she can remove herself from the wounds that have been inflicted on her; if she can take her focus off her husband to focus on God instead; if she can catch hold of the truth that her prayers are so extremely powerful, then she's going to be able to rise up and do battle for something she loves and cares about—and hopefully that is her marriage and her husband. It might help her to be more merciful toward her husband if she sees him in the same light as she would her child who's being tormented by somebody. He is God's child, and he's being tormented by Satan."

How Spiritual Problems Start

"There are two culprits when a Christian is no longer walking according to Scripture. Either there is direct demonic involvement in the form of oppression, or the person has allowed the flesh to run rampant and they have yielded to the flesh instead of to the Holy Spirit. Usually it starts with the flesh and turns into a spiritual oppression because the enemy quickly picks up on the loosening of the fleshly desires and then starts to build a stronghold in that person's life."

How a Wife Can Identify the Existence of a Stronghold in Her Husband

"A stronghold is spiritually discerned. As you notice things that are offensive to you in your husband, pray and ask God to show you if it is a stronghold. Signs may include mood swings; behavior that seems out of character for your husband; changes in his behavior or attitude; inappropriate preoccupations; addictions to sensual desires; extreme negativity, stubbornness, control, or self-pity."

How to Pray

"First realize that, as a believer, you have the spiritual authority. Submit your husband and your marital problems to God. Submit your own life to God. Once you have done these things, you as a believer have authority over all the power of the enemy, and when you take this authority to come against and bind the enemy, the enemy has no choice but to leave."

Binding the Enemy

"Satan, I bind you in the name of Jesus Christ and take authority over you and command you to be gone from _____ in Jesus' name. I command you to be gone from _____'s life, from his mind, his emotions, from his actions, and his very thoughts. And Satan I cast down every thought that you would try to put into _____'s mind. I cast down everything that is contrary to the will of God."

Frequency

"It doesn't hurt to apply a fresh 'bloodline' over your husband's life a few times a day to keep the enemy at bay. Particularly if your husband has been a spiritual leader, the enemy is going to probe and probe and probe. Someone needs to stand in the gap resisting, resisting, resisting, to cover your husband with the blood of Christ and asking God to build a hedge around his life."

Binding Satan in another person may be only temporary. Deep strongholds can be eliminated only when the person himself willingly submits to God's deliverance and then walks out his freedom by practicing scriptural principles in his life. But when we enter into battle on our spouse's behalf, and if we do it often enough, even several times a day, we can help eliminate satanic strongholds. If one's spouse is free from Satan's deception for a time, he may be receptive to God's voice and the words of other Christians, which can ultimately lead to his spiritual restoration and healing.

> *Greater is he that is in you,*
> *than he that is in the world.*
>
> —1 JOHN 4:4 KJV

BURNED POTATOES

> *Be made new in the attitude of your minds; and*
> *... put on the new self, created to be like God in*
> *true righteousness and holiness.*
>
> —EPHESIANS 4:23–24

*L*ast night while making dinner, I burned the potatoes. The steak was tough, and I put too much salt on the string beans. It was a pretty lousy meal.

But tonight I'm beginning over. I plan to cook the steak on a hotter fire to break down the fibers. I'll keep a closer eye on the potatoes, and go lighter on seasoning the veggies. It's a new day and a new opportunity to do things right.

Byron and Suzy's marriage had been in crisis for eighteen months. They had gone through a short separation, and their reconciliation had been volatile.

"We'd never had a fight before a year or so ago," Byron announced to the long-time friends gathered together over dinner.

Suzy rolled her eyes. "Because I was a doormat," she said. "Because I always just gave in to you."

"You seemed to want me to make the decisions."

"Yeah. I did," she said thoughtfully. "That's probably true. Then, if things went wrong, I wouldn't be at fault."

"We've been married a long time," Byron resumed, "and this was the pattern of our lives for so long. I think when you get to a certain age, you come to a place where you are able to look back at your whole experience and suddenly the light breaks through; you see something needs to change." He looked over at his wife. "Suzy saw it first."

"You mean because of Valerie," Suzy shot back with a lift of her eyebrows.

It was the lightning rod that had flashed between them for a long time. For more than a year Byron had blamed the counselor, Valerie, for upsetting Suzy and creating all their problems.

This time, however, he didn't react. He didn't even cringe. "Valerie may have been a part of it, but you were the first one to see we needed a change. And now, today, I see it. And our marriage will never be the same."

"It will be better," she said.

"Yes," he agreed. "It will."

Before today Byron had always let the lightning rod burn in his mind. He'd react negatively and then throw the issue back to her, an active spark in their heated marital debates. But today Byron had neutralized it. He'd done something different. Instead of treating the words as a lightning rod, he had weighed them in his mind and let them cool down. They couldn't harm him unless he let them. He reacted differently, and the rest of the conversation spun out in a new direction.

In their book *Overcoming Relationship Impasses*, psychologists Barry Duncan and Joseph Rock explain that every sequence of communication between individuals provides the opportunity to either maintain things as they are or redefine them. One small change in a certain area can cause a positive ripple effect. Either person in a marriage can move the relationship in a different direction by interrupting a disagreeable pattern of communication that has become a habit. Duncan and Rock refer to this as "causal circles in relationships" (Insight, 1991).

As you travel this difficult road, you don't know what will happen tomorrow. You want to see tomorrow flower into something beautiful and new. And it can. But only if you do things differently. Maybe the last conversation turned into a yelling match. It was a disaster. But if you plan ahead, your next encounter can be different.

If we want a delicious steak dinner, we don't cook it the same way we did when it turned out tasteless and tough. If we want a better marriage, we learn to respond in new ways.

And isn't that what God challenges us to do when he tells us to "be made new in the attitude of our minds"? Never does God want us to remain static. Constantly he prods us on to newness and growth.

God wants to reveal truths to you, not only as to how to heal your marriage but how to heal yourself. He wants to change you by touching your heart and the deeper parts of your being. He wants you to follow him into uncharted territories.

Give God free rein. Let him make you new in the attitude of your mind. Let go of the old habits, the old thinking, the old you. Let God show you what changes to make in your next encounter with your husband. Listen to his voice as he leads you. Read his Word. Ask God to help you identify the circular web that is sapping the energy from your marriage. When you do, you can turn those plain boiled potatoes into *pommes frites*.

> *Create in me a clean heart, O God;*
> *and renew a right spirit within me.*
> —Psalm 51:10 KJV

A Healing Salve

> *The Lord is not slow in keeping his promise,*
> *as some understand slowness. He is patient*
> *with you, not wanting anyone to perish,*
> *but everyone to come to repentance.*
> —2 Peter 3:9

*I*n the movie *The Horse Whisperer,* a horse named Pilgrim is seriously injured in an accident, leaving him physically, mentally, and emotionally scarred. His vet, believing the animal is beyond help, recommends putting the animal out of his misery. But unwilling to give up on her horse, Pilgrim's owner solicits help from a horse whisperer, a man with an unusually deep affinity and understanding of horses. Even though he, too, feels Pilgrim may be too severely traumatized to recover, he agrees to help.

Attempting to soothe the horse and earn his trust, the horse whisperer works with Pilgrim but is unable to curb his rebellion. When the horse becomes agitated and upset, the man lets him go without trying to hinder him.

Free to go where he wants, Pilgrim races into the pasture and stands a considerable way off. In silence the horse whisperer sits, watching and waiting. For hours neither moves. Finally, Pilgrim turns and looks back to see that the man is still there, then whinnies and begins drifting back toward him. A few feet shy, however, Pilgrim stops. The two lock eyes. Without stirring, the horse whisperer waits silently. Pilgrim steps closer, hesitates, then again moves in the man's direction. When he is finally in the man's presence, the horse lowers his head and nudges the man's arm, at last trusting the horse whisperer to lead him through the healing process.

If you have an emotionally or spiritually scarred spouse, you may have to be like the horse whisperer. The only thing you may be able to do right now is to sit and wait. Your mate may run away and remain distant for a while, expecting you to take some kind of action. But when he sees that you are not pursuing him, not running from him, not creating a new set of circumstances for him to deal with—when he sees you waiting patiently in love to allow him time to heal, he may come around to open up the communication lines again.

This is what God does with his children when they stray. He wants those he loves to return to him. He sits in the field and waits while we run off to exercise our freedom.

We often wonder, "Why, Lord, must this suffering last so long?" But God knows how long it will take for the necessary changes to take place. Healing takes time. Things may even get worse before they get better. God may now be asking you to draw close, to be in partnership with him as together you watch and wait for your mate's healing.

> God, help me exercise self-control by reining in my tongue and my desire for action. Your Word says that long-suffering is a fruit of the spirit, but you know how strenuously I resist the idea of sitting in pain. Give me the patience to wait, the wisdom to know when words are useless, and the self-control to keep silent when they are. Finally, Lord, give me the strength to be your instrument for my husband's healing, if that is your desire, and enough love to keep me strong when tempted to give up.

SHADOWS

The green of the grass looks greener
in the morning
when the sun splits the shadows
and side by side the sunlight and the shadow lie.

Hope rises within me as
the sun continues its ascent
for unless clouds come along to intercede
before it reaches its apex,
the shadows will be forced to scatter,

finding refuge solely beneath drooping branches
and the rectilinear backstop of the fence.

I look to the sky
searching the edges of the horizon
and gathering hues above
looking for the promise of this day.
But despite the prediction of weather forecasters,
the secrets of today unfold in minute by minute
revelation.
We must watch and wait.

When Beautiful Things Die

*I tell you the truth, unless a kernel of wheat falls to
the ground and dies, it remains only a single seed.
But if it dies, it produces many seeds. The man who
loves his life will lose it, while the man who hates
his life in this world will keep it for eternal life.*

—John 12:24–25

*I*t's hard to watch something die, particularly if it's something
you considered a thing of beauty and fulfillment. You want to
fight to save it, just like you want to save your marriage from death.

Perhaps some of you will look back at your marriage and
remember nothing but painful, negative things. But others
remember the good times, the love connection that was supposed
to be there always. You remember that original commitment and
agonize over the loss. You lash out at what is happening, hoping

that by doing so, you can force it to go away. You feel death at your door and push back.

With every ounce of strength and will, you fight to save your marriage.

We as Christians believe that when we die, we'll be transformed, and our new spiritual bodies will begin life afresh in the presence of God. It's just like when a caterpillar goes into a cocoon and appears to be dead but in time emerges as a beautiful butterfly. By dying it can live again.

Even though it breaks your heart, this may be what is happening to your marriage. The death of a marriage does not necessarily mean you will not have a love relationship with your spouse again. It simply means that circumstances have taken you to the point where your marriage can no longer be sustained by the original breath of life that framed it. But the encouraging thing is that even when the body of the *marriage* is dead, the *people* are still alive; their hearts are still beating, and new life in a new marriage is possible—even with the same two people.

But before the new life can begin, the old one must finish dying. We have to let it go so God can peacefully come in and excavate the dying roots and crumbling ruins. We must remove our heart from the hand of the spouse who has so abused it and give it into the keeping of God. This may require a time alone to heal the wounds and refresh our spirit, to let God's love wash through us and give us eyes to see our true self—the one he loves—not the one our spouse rejected. It's an opportunity for us to stop seeing ourselves through the eyes of our spouse and begin seeing ourselves anew through the eyes of God.

At first it will be scary as you place the security of your future solely in God's hands. The flesh of our fingers can't reach out and touch him. Our ears can't hear his voice cutting audibly through the airwaves. But he is here. And he is strong. He can make you strong. As you rest in the security of his love, one day perhaps you will be able to look at your husband with new eyes. And one day your husband may see the new person in you—deeper, stronger, more compassionate, and eventually more forgiving.

Then perhaps—if you let him—God can fashion a brand-new marriage between you and your spouse.

Old things are passed away; behold,
all things are become new.

—2 CORINTHIANS 5:17 KJV

A CHANGE OF DIRECTION

Show me your ways, O LORD,
teach me your paths; guide me in your
truth and teach me, for you are God my Savior,
and my hope is in you all day long.

—PSALM 25:4–5

Lights sparkled on the Christmas tree amid the gaiety of laughter. Brightly colored wrapping paper littered the floor of the living room as the pile of presents gradually dwindled. Two delightfully witty young men who were dating my daughters added to the merriment. But Christmas day was different this year. My mother, my two daughters, and I were there as usual, but my husband was not. It was the first Christmas in more than twenty years that we had been apart. And although there was an empty nook in one corner of my heart, I didn't miss him. I was content.

For this Christmas I was living in the truth. No pretense from him that he was happy in the marriage. No walking on eggshells by me to make sure he did not erupt. I was accepting the reality of what was, and it felt extremely good. I could be a whole person. I could laugh. I could live life without him, and I was not falling apart.

It was two months earlier, after a counseling appointment, that I had last seen him. "I'll call you later," he'd said as I hurried toward my car.

Without looking back at him, I nodded with a dull sense of hopelessness as the counseling session continued to echo through my mind. He had just told me he could not make a commitment to me. After being separated for a year and a half, suffering through the ins and outs of painful reconciliation attempts, going to two counselors—and after he *said* he wanted to get back together—I didn't understand what was happening. What were we doing? What was the point of going any further? *If there wasn't a commitment, how could there be a marriage?*

I knew even before I touched the car door handle that I would not want to talk to him when he called. The dead weight pulling at my heart told me so. There was no point. And so I filled up the holidays by spending time with friends and other family members while trying to erase him from my thoughts.

I would like to say I was at peace, but it was more of an acceptance of where I was—like standing at the end of a pier and knowing if I walked any further, I would plunge into the water. God was still sovereign, but there was no more maneuvering on my part. God had to do it all. And I needed to let go completely so he could do it—without my help.

Time Apart

In my particular story, physical as well as emotional distance was necessary at this point. Although it's not a course I would casually recommend to others, if the pain lingers so long it becomes overwhelming and feels as though it will pull you under, distancing yourself may be the only way. Proverbs 4:23 says, "Guard your heart, for it is the wellspring of life." When a marital crisis winds its way through mazes that seem to have no exit and no resolution, you may come to a crossroads where in order to guard your heart and see things clearly you feel the need to consider other alternatives and step out in a new direction.

For some, that may mean disentangling yourself from your husband emotionally, taking a deep breath, and walking away with God so he can heal you and make you into a whole person. Distance and space may provide the perspective to help you move beyond denial to acceptance of the truth of where you are, without bitterness and without your heart sinking into caverns of despair. It can be a transition moment when God bolsters your inner person to give you strength.

At the beginning of his ministry, Jesus had a transition moment when he went off into the wilderness for forty days to separate himself from the world and be alone with God. During this time, God drew him close and strengthened him with love and power. Later, Jesus often withdrew from the confusion of the crowds to get apart with God so he could seek his Father's guidance and be renewed.

If, at some point on your difficult journey, you feel distance is needed to save yourself and perhaps your marriage, remember to keep your eyes on Jesus as you allow his Word to seep into your heart and strengthen you. Stay continually in his presence and pray for your husband to become the man God wants him to be. Seek wise counsel from encouraging Christian friends and maybe from a professional counselor. In time the hope that is in God will buoy you up and guide your steps in truth and wisdom.

Keep in mind that each situation is entirely different. Yours is not the same as mine. Let God guide you into the light of truth with a rhythm and pace that is uniquely your own.

> O God guide my steps. Show me your truth.
> Heal the brokenness of my spirit and make
> me whole. Don't let me run ahead of you, and
> don't let me lag behind. Keep me near.

My hope is in you all day long.
For your love is ever before me, and I walk
continually in your truth.

—PSALM 25:5; 26:3

THE QUIETNESS OF YOUR HEART

If you abide in me, and my words abide in you,
ask whatever you will, and it shall be done for you.

—JOHN 15:7 RSV

*W*hen your heart is quiet before God, when you have immersed yourself in the Scriptures, when you are sharing and listening to encouraging Christian friends, when you are shutting out the noise of discouragement, you will hear the quiet whispers of God speaking to your heart. And in the quietness of your heart you can find the truth.

It is that simple. And it is that hard. Our mind spins through the past, plowing through memories of wrongs and regrets. Our emotions flare up, warning us either to fight or flee. Pain forms a casing of scar tissue around our heart, which prevents us from being sensitive to the things of God. We hold on to the pain instead of giving it all over to our Lord, and it settles in layers around our heart. Nothing gets in or out.

But when we give all that pain to our Savior and allow our heart to be vulnerable to him, he will pour his Spirit into it and make it sensitive to his voice. Then as we listen to our heart, he can show us the way.

As you search for answers along the winding road, as you peek into the shadows for clues and question passersby for directions, confusion shuts out answers. The signposts along the way continue to elude you. You still don't know the right thing to do, the right way to go.

Rather than listening to the clamor and the noise of the advice-givers, listen to your heart. If you abide with God and seek refuge within the shelter of his arms, he will show you the simple truth that dwells beneath the veil of confusion which shrouds the world around you. The secret is in the abiding.

Somewhere within your heart God has planted the truth that you seek. But you must be quiet before him and listen to what he says to you. When we abide in Jesus and let his words seep into our hearts, our wills become fashioned by his will; our desires become his. Our hearts are fused with God's.

Let God lead you like his partner in the dance as you stay continually sensitive to his movements and subtle nuances of direction. And trust God for the patience and courage to follow through with what you need to do.

As you stay close to God, the Holy Spirit gently draws you forward, guiding you step by step in the direction you should go. In the stillness you know what he wants you to do for this particular moment, and you feel the sweetness of his presence, the lightness of his touch as you move with him through the coming days. His voice may never again be as sweet and real to you as it is now. He is a companion, friend, husband, comfort, and love that will not let you go. And when you look back at this time, you may realize that the lightness you feel is actually the weightlessness of being carried in his arms as you leave behind trouble and turmoil and press on toward the treasure he has in store for you.

> Dear Lord, keep me ever near you. Tune my heart to yours. Let me hear the whispers of your Holy Spirit as he guides me through each day. And, Lord, show me the truth. Let me trust the truth that is in you, that you have hidden in my heart, that you reveal in the light of your Word.

FROM LOVE AND BACK AGAIN

J'm flattered by your invitation. But, no—I don't think so—not right now anyway." Kimberly cleared her throat and ran her fingers through her short curls. "Maybe I'll take a rain check." Slowly she laid the receiver of the phone on the hook, then continued to stare at it as if seeing a ghost.

A date with Aaron? After eight years? She shivered.

He sounded so nice on the phone. He'd been friendly lately when she saw him at the children's soccer games too. And what a change that was! But—a date? Dinner? After being divorced for eight years?

Aaron's face loomed into her mind, not the pleasant face of the man she'd just been talking to, but the angry face she'd seen so often in the past. The face that had frightened her and made her want to run away—which she eventually did.

She saw him reprimanding her, pointing to a list he'd put on the refrigerator. "Why can't you get these things done, Kim? You're a stay-at-home mom. Count the number of minutes you're at home, the hours. Why can't you do this? You're just not arranging your time right."

Kim's mind would freeze. He was so logical. Maybe he was right. So she'd try. But she'd always fail. She was taking good care of the babies, she was sure of that. It was just hard to get everything done on his list.

She shuddered as she thought back to that time early in their marriage. She should have stood up to him. That's what her friends told her later. But she couldn't deal with confrontation. She simply did not have the self-confidence to assert herself in a healthy manner.

But after she went back to work and he bought a restaurant, it got worse. In an attempt to supplement their income, Aaron not only taught college by day but worked every evening selling pizza. He drank coffee continually to make it through his sixteen-hour days. His patience, which was already minimal, became almost nonexistent. His temper flared frequently. Eventually she came to a point where she could no longer live with his temper and controlling ways. She filed for divorce. Although they both went to great lengths to protect their children, their divorce was far from friendly.

Kimberly removed her hand from the phone, got up, and went to the kitchen for a soda. The sound of Aaron's voice as she'd heard it on the phone a few minutes earlier chimed through her ears. It had been a nice conversation. They'd talked for almost an hour.

Images of happier times took shape in her mind. She saw him playing softball with their kids. Saw the gleam in his eyes when he surprised her with plane tickets to New York, a city she'd always dreamed of visiting. Yes, there'd been some very good times.

Kimberly went to the telephone and called her friend Jeannette. Having been married three times—the last time for thirty years—Jeannette seemed a good person to ask for advice.

"I told him no," Kimberly said. "He said he wanted to bring up the subject of reconciling."

"Wait a minute," Jeannette said. "If you go out to dinner, you may find you don't even like each other, and that'll be that. Or you may find a spark of something you had before that is still alive."

"I don't trust Aaron," Kimberly said. "What if he does something to embarrass me?"

"You don't think he'd start yelling at you in a public place, do you?"

"I don't know."

"Give it a chance, Kim. You're in public. It's unlikely he's going to do anything like that. And unless you give it a chance, you'll never know if you could put it back together."

"I don't know if I want to put it back together. I've started dating again, you know."

"Listen, if you get married to somebody else, like I have, there is a huge difference. Your husband is not your kids' father. It's your kids, his kids—he won't have the same feelings for Sara and Jeffrey—like Aaron does."

She woke Aaron up when she called him back later that night. "I'd like to collect on that rain check if you still want to go out," she said. They talked for another hour and a half and arranged dinner together a week later.

During the following week Kimberly searched her heart and mind. Was getting back with Aaron really possible? Only if he met certain conditions, she decided. She couldn't possibly go back to what they had before. They would have to start fresh. They'd have to go to counseling and work seriously on their relationship. Kimberly got out a piece of paper and began to list her conditions:

1. Go to counseling.
2. No more displays of temper. Aaron must agree to learn anger management skills.
3. Mutual respect.

She looked at what she had written so far and smiled. This was so unlike her. In the past she would never have thought this far ahead to make such a list. She'd really grown up in the past eight years.

She grimaced as she remembered the first time she tried to balance a checkbook after the divorce. Her counselor had helped too by drilling it into her head that she, Kimberly, was an okay person. She was worthwhile.

But it wasn't until she went back to church that she had been able to turn another very important corner. Anger and resentment had churned up her insides. She hated Aaron. The church singles group she attended studied a book on forgiveness. It said people who hurt usually don't do it intentionally but lack the tools to communicate and behave effectively. She thought about Aaron's angry outbursts, his frustration and inability to put his feelings to one side so he could deal with issues calmly. *Maybe Aaron was doing the best he could. Maybe he just didn't have the tools to control his temper. Maybe that was it.*

Gradually, as she had been able to accept the fact that no amount of anger on her part would change him or anything in their circumstances, she was able to let go and forgive.

Kimberly looked down at her list and made another notation.

4. I want to continue going to church, whether Aaron goes or not.

Aaron had chosen one of their favorite restaurants overlooking the bay for dinner. The quiet, rustic atmosphere was warm and intimate. As Kimberly settled into the chair opposite Aaron, she saw a glow in his eyes she hadn't seen for years.

"I've been watching you lately, Kim," Aaron said. "I like your new self-confidence. You seem much more your own person."

"I guess I've grown up a lot," Kimberly said. She spread her napkin in her lap and opened the menu. "I've enjoyed how you seem to be treating me with respect when I've seen you at the kids' games and things. And I enjoyed our conversations over the phone."

"I did too."

"I was really surprised when you asked me out to dinner. What happened?"

"Remember when I took the kids on a weekend vacation on the river with my cousin Betty and rented a houseboat? Betty saw how unhappy I was and asked me about it. I couldn't give her an answer. I was in a real funk."

Kimberly remembered the trip. It wasn't long after his eighteen-month marriage with another woman had ended.

"Betty said, 'I'm not going to talk to you for the rest of the weekend until you can tell me what would make you happy.'

"Well, she made me think, and for the next twenty-four hours I tried to remember what had made me happy in the past. And every time I started thinking, it was 'Kim.'" His eyes widened to mimic his surprise. "Your name kept popping into my mind.

"I started remembering when we were in college together, when we first married, when the kids were born. I'd shake my head—no, no, that couldn't possibly be true. And I'd start thinking some more, trying to remember when I'd been the happiest, and again it was you."

A lightness washed through Kimberly's body. She could feel her lips curling up at the corners. She felt her heart skip a beat.

Aaron sighed, sat back in his seat, and looked at her. "And then about the same time, Sara confronted me with the fervor and conviction only a teenage daughter can muster. She told me she was embarrassed to have her friends around me because of my lack of patience, my temper. Two women have left me for the same reason, and now my daughter says this. Maybe there *is* something about me...."

Kimberly laughed. "Yes, I guess that might send a message."

"As I told you on the phone, I'd like to talk about the possibility of reconciling."

Kimberly reached into her purse and brought out her list. "Aaron, there are certain conditions you'd have to agree to before I could even consider reconciling. And it's a long list."

As they talked over the items she'd jotted down, she sensed a newness between them. He'd changed, as she had. They talked about who they had each become and how they had gotten there. They discussed what they were looking for in a committed relationship. He agreed to everything on her list. The warmth in her heart grew into a spark. She couldn't believe the feelings that were rising up within her. She had hated him. And now.... Where were these feelings of love coming from? But they had been married for more than seventeen years. And there had been many happy times together. It was all coming back.

When he took her back to her apartment, the spark ignited. They fell into each other's arms. There was no question about their future together. They were in love again.

Both now motivated to develop the kind of behaviors that would make a new marriage together work, they went back to counseling. A year later, on their former anniversary date, they remarried. That was in 1986. It was a whole new beginning. Kimberly saw Aaron become more tolerant. When something upset him, he talked it out and got over it. He was more willing to consider his own culpability in causing problems. With a new self-confidence, Kimberly learned to assert herself by expressing her individual thoughts and desires. "I thought we always had to agree on everything or things weren't good," she says now. "But there are times we just have to agree to disagree."

Today they have been married as long as they were the first time. With a new level of friendship, they have a whole new way of communicating. Kimberly has become a better listener and although she still has trouble confronting him when something bothers her, she's improving. "We're still a work in progress," she says. "But it's wonderful."

Part 5

A RESTORED HEART

*I press on toward the goal to
win the prize for which God has
called me heavenward in Christ Jesus.*

—PHILIPPIANS 3:14

THE JOURNEY

Then the angel showed me the river of the
water of life, as clear as crystal, flowing
from the throne of God and of the Lamb down
the middle of the great street of the city.

—REVELATION 22:1

As I walked along the beach, I looked out over a large expanse of blue where sky and ocean merged into one. Puffs of white clouds billowed above the horizon while at the shoreline waves broke into streams of white foam. Wisps of clouds floating and shimmering gossamer in the sunlight against a brilliant blue sky infused the scene with an ethereal sense.

An endless expanse of time and space stretched out before me, and I envisioned what it would look like to walk into eternity. I could see Jesus standing there in the delicate, white clouds before me, reaching out his hands and welcoming me into his heaven.

The peace and beauty of that day reminded me what it would be like then. I was alone walking on the beach. When the time came for me to walk into eternity, I would also walk alone—just as I was right then. A warmth flowed through me as I sensed what the beauty of that walk would be like—the Lord welcoming me home, the sunlight shining from everywhere.

No one would go with me. It would be my own private journey—my own walk down the aisle—like the bride going to meet the groom. Even if I was married, my husband would not go with me on this journey. He would take his own. Regardless of what happened here on earth, what relationships we had, how close we were to another, or how entwined our lives were; regardless of how dependent we were on them or they on us; regardless of how someone had wronged us—when we take that walk into eternity, we go alone.

On that day, at that moment, it will be just me and God. It won't matter what someone did to me or if I was happy or unhappy. All that will matter then is whether my response was fashioned by God or by myself. Did I respond by taking a step closer to God or moving away? Did I retreat into myself or did I retreat into the heart of the Lord? Did I open myself up to the quiet whispers of God or withdraw into the hard and lonely darkness of my pain?

I lift up my eyes to you,
to you whose throne is in heaven.

—Psalm 123:1

Against the Undertow

One standing alone can be attacked and
defeated, but two can stand back-to-back
and conquer; three is even better, for a
triple-braided cord is not easily broken.

—Ecclesiastes 4:12 TLB

The waves undulated with a refreshing vigor as they splashed over our bodies and swept us along in their current. With the blistering sun breaking through the hazy Southern California sky overhead, the cool salt water was a wonderful reprieve from the intense August heat.

Stopping to float and drift in the rolling surf, I looked back at the crowds on Huntington Beach, where earlier in the day a number of us from our church youth group had laid our towels on the coarse sand. Even from that distance, I could have seen the red warning flag in the distance cautioning against the undertow, but I didn't.

The full, long waves were perfect for body surfing. All day we dove through the mounting swells, rode them in, then splashed back into the depths. The shallow water extended far into the ocean, and in our youthful enthusiasm, we wandered recklessly out beyond the waves with no thought of danger.

At length we decided to rejoin our group on the beach. Turning toward shore, however, we were alarmed to discover a steely undertow pushing against us, a solid wall of water relentless in its determination to prevent our forward movement. The three of us strained forward with every ounce of strength, but an hour later we were still alarmingly far from shore. Scanning the coastline for friends and familiar landmarks, we realized we had drifted so far down the beach that our friends were nowhere in sight. We were on our own and feeling desperately weak.

As Alice and I pressed on, our friend Donna began to lag behind, then completely stopped and stood in the swirling waters, a look of exhaustion lengthening across her sunburned face. "I can't go on. I can't take another step," she cried.

Alice and I looked at her, aghast. Fear surged through my already weary frame.

"You can make it!" Alice coaxed. "Hold onto our hands."

"I can't," she moaned. Her eyes were dull. Her listless body already appeared to drift in the fierce heaviness of water.

"We'll make it," I said. "Just don't give up. Hold on."

The next hour was one of the most physically draining in my life. Amid silent, and sometimes audible prayers, Alice and I mustered every ounce of strength to drag and pull Donna along behind while stretching our inner resolve to find the stamina to continue moving forward ourselves. Struggling for the energy to shove our bodies into the oppressive weight of water, we were forced to take frequent rests to regain our strength.

The long awaited moment finally came when the fierce current flattening itself against us gave way. It was like being loosed from a vice. The thrill of relief and a rush of thanks to God swept through me. We had made it. We had all made it— together.

Exhilarated but weak, we trudged up the beach to rejoin our group. That's when we spotted the red flag.

That day I learned that sometimes on our life journey there are interludes when we need to hang back with someone in the midst of a strong undertow so the other person can make it to safety. Yes, we might be able to find refuge faster if we go on alone, but God did not put us in marriages so we could *make it alone*.

A lifetime is a long time. We will all have seasons when we are weak and need the other to be strong for us. At other times we will both be robust enough to storm through the undertow together.

Ask God if this may be one of those seasons when he wants you to hang back in prayer for your husband while continuing to push forward against the spiritual and emotional undertow that could easily drag both of you under.

And while holding on together, consider what red flags the two of you may have missed along the way.

But the wisdom that comes from heaven is
first of all pure and full of quiet gentleness. Then
it is peace-loving and courteous. It allows
discussion and is willing to yield to others; it
is full of mercy and good deeds. It is
wholehearted and straightforward and sincere.
—JAMES 3:17 TLB

STANDING FIRM

Stand firm then, with the belt of truth buckled
around your waist, with the breastplate of righ-
teousness in place, and with your feet fitted with
the readiness that comes from the gospel of peace.
—EPHESIANS 6:14–15

J'm not a football fan. But for years I have faithfully donned an orange-and-blue shirt, hung orange-and-blue flags in the windows behind the TV, and watched the Florida Gators battle other SEC teams, a dutiful wife watching without completely comprehending the aura of the game. What I do enjoy, however, are the personalities behind the game—the interviews, interpersonal relationships, and analogies to life I occasionally glean from it.

While watching a game one afternoon, two football commentators discussed a touchdown made when one player had pounded his way past a pair of grappling, bruising defensive players.

"He took a lot of punishment from those two tackles," one commentator observed.

"That's how you get a touchdown. You're going to take the punishment anyway whether you hold on to the ball or not, so you might as well hold on to the ball and get the touchdown," the other replied.

In life as well as football, we often "have to take the punishment anyway." We're going to suffer no matter what. When we're in a crisis, no matter where we run, we'll still be in the crisis—whether we hold onto the ball, drop it, or fall down and let life's burdens topple on top of us. So we might as well "hold on to the ball and get the touchdown."

Right now you are still standing. You are not defeated. As you have spent time in prayer, read the Scriptures, and talked to Christian friends, you have finally come to a place you feel God has brought you. You may still have no idea where all this is leading; the future remains unknown. But continue to listen for his voice, assured that when it is time to move on, you will know. Until then you are in this place right now, and it is here that you stand.

"But," you might ask, "how do I stand?

Ephesians 6:14–15 tells us to stand firm with the belt of truth, the breastplate of righteousness, and with our feet ready with Christ's peace. If we are living by the truth of Jesus Christ and being honest with God and ourselves, we are girded correctly around the waist with the belt of truth. If we are resisting temptation, taking Jesus' righteousness upon ourselves and "meeting the requirements" of the relationship with our husband by praying for them and treating them as God leads, we are protected by the breastplate of righteousness.

Once we have these first two pieces of armor in place, and if we pray for our husbands, God will probably show us something about our attitudes. Perhaps we need to replace an over-dependence on our husbands with a complete dependence on God. Or perhaps we need to develop a more gentle and receptive attitude. When God makes us new in the attitude of our mind, we will be ready with God's peace when the time comes for us to move, regardless of the direction he takes us.

In 2 Corinthians 4:8–9, Paul describes what could be the spiritual equivalent of a successful quarterback. "We are hard pressed on every side, but not crushed; perplexed, but not in despair; persecuted, but not abandoned; struck down, but not destroyed." Like the football player fighting through his opposition, Paul's description is a picture of strength and perseverance. Unlike the football player, however, our ability to stand during our crisis does not depend on our own strength. "We have this treasure in jars of clay," says 2 Corinthians 4:7, "to show that this all-surpassing power is from God and not from us." It is in our weakness that he is strong. As we continue listening to God's voice, we can stand where we are until he leads us on.

So I picture you standing there, the ball in your hands. You are badgered on every side. You can give in and drop the ball. Or you can stay on your feet and run—maybe to just make a first down or maybe all the way down the field to score a touchdown. But for now you are standing, and the ball is still in play, even though you do not know which way to run. The coach on the sidelines is telling you what to do. Look to him for the signal. Listen to him above the roar of the crowd. Hold onto the ball and stand.

You need to persevere so that when you have done the will of God, you will receive what he has promised.
—Hebrews 10:36

EXTINGUISHING THE ARROWS

*Take up the shield of faith, with which you can
extinguish all the flaming arrows of the evil
one.... And pray in the Spirit on all occasions.*

—EPHESIANS 6:16, 18

One of the scary things about following God is that sometimes we don't understand the importance of remaining in his presence to prevent Satan from catching us off guard—because it is at those unguarded moments that Satan loves to attack. And his attacks can be exquisitely deceptive. I believe one of Satan's favorite strategies is to attack right when God has set a blessing in motion or right when God is about to demolish a stronghold. Before we can actually see what God is doing, Satan will attempt to demoralize us to discourage us from pursuing a direction that is about to bear fruit.

Two years into our separation, my husband and I had begun dating on a friendly basis. We would go to a movie or out to dinner on the weekend, then go to church together on Sunday. Although it was a positive move forward, my heart still ached at the emotional distance between us. One Saturday night we were sitting in the family room talking to our daughter Laura when she unexpectedly invited her father to go to a new church with her the next morning. He eagerly accepted, and the two of them made plans.

I was tempted to complain, to let them know that I felt excluded. But mustering all my newly learned self-control, I said nothing.

The next morning, after my husband and daughter left for church, the familiar shadow of depression crept over me as I descended the stairs for some coffee. But somewhere between the bedroom and the kitchen, the Holy Spirit got my attention. Instead of succumbing to Satan's tempting snare, I made a detour to the family room, put on a praise album, and spent the rest of the morning on my knees praying.

That church service turned out to be the beginning of my husband's spiritual reawakening, which became a most important reminder to me that God is God and I am not. Whenever I think about that Sunday morning, I marvel that if I had allowed my feelings to take control and interfere with God's purpose, if I had complained, if I had wallowed in self-pity, I could have missed the incredible blessing he had in store for us.

Satan does not want us to be at peace. Satan does not want our marriages to be restored. Satan does not want us to find victory and spiritual restoration. So, very possibly, right at the time when a breakthrough is about to take place, he will whisper doubts in our minds. He will suggest that we focus on something to discourage us, something to make us conclude that everything is hopeless so we will take some action that will put a halt to God's momentum forward. This is called temptation.

Satan will tempt us to take control of the situation according to our own human understanding, to go our own way, to react out of the flesh, to give up. "Did God really say, 'You must not eat from any tree in the garden'?" Satan asked Eve (Gen. 3:1). Satan knew God's command did not include *all* the trees of the garden, but he skewed God's instruction just enough to throw Eve off guard so she would start conversing with Satan. Once he had her attention, he could begin to manipulate the conversation so that she focused on what Satan was saying rather than on what God had said.

We must never take our attention off the Lord. We must never give Satan the opportunity to discourage us. Remember that Satan is a liar. What looks discouraging may not be what it appears. For all we know, the very situation we are bemoaning may be a part of God's plan to bring us our victory.

Boldly hold up that shield of faith between you and Satan so his lies and flaming arrows cannot touch your heart or deflate your spirit. Keep your eyes on Jesus. Pray always. Trust that God knows what must transpire before he can give you the good gifts you desire.

Therefore put on the full armor of God,
so that when the day of evil comes, you may be
able to stand your ground, and after you
have done everything, to stand.

—EPHESIANS 6:13

GREAT MYSTERIES

Forgive your brother from your heart.

—MATTHEW 18:35

*I*n 1997, the whole country watched Kathie Lee Gifford as she was forced to live out in the national media the private pain from her husband's adulterous behavior. Her husband's videotaped unfaithfulness was compounded a hundredfold by the public disgrace it brought upon her. Speculation was rampant as to what she would do.

Then the whole world watched in amazement while Kathie Lee let God's love and grace flow through her as a healing balm to bless her husband with the gift of forgiveness and restoration.

Separated at the time and trying to pick my way through the remaining pieces of my own marriage, I pored over every news account as her saga of inner strength unfolded. Instead of allowing her humiliation to control her reactions, she continued to face the cameras on her daily TV show with poise and restraint. Instead of divorcing, she and her husband issued a joint statement asking that their privacy be respected. With help from a counselor, she set appropriate boundaries to give her husband the chance to regain her trust, and together they began the hard work of reconciliation.

As she lived out her Christian faith with all the blemishes and intimate details of her life exposed to public view, Kathie Lee Gifford became an example to women everywhere of the power of God's grace and forgiveness. Untold numbers of people were touched by her Christian testimony. God crystallized the excruciating pain she suffered and turned it into diamonds for his kingdom as women like me learned how to forgive.

Forgiveness is one of the most painful decisions we can make. We know that somehow we're supposed to forgive, but when we step right up to it, we feel as though we're being asked to turn ourselves inside out, tear out our hearts, and give them into the hands of our enemy.

What does it mean to forgive? And how do we do it? Does God really expect us to forgive?

As I watched Kathie Lee live out forgiveness in her marriage, I took baby steps to heal my own. I knew forgiveness was foundational to the Christian faith. I knew that Jesus forgave the people even as they mocked him and watched him die a terrible death. Every time I prayed the Lord's Prayer, I asked God to forgive me the same way I forgave others.

But as I walked this path, I discovered that forgiveness is not a cruel demand that a sadistic God imposes on the hurting. It is the painful but healing door to freedom. It is surgery on the heart that extracts the poison of bitterness so we can move forward into a healthy life. Forgiveness is a choice we make intentionally, not because we just want to put the memory behind us, because we've been told we must, or because we think it will cause God to give us what we want. We choose to forgive because we recognize the tremendous mercy and power in God's forgiveness *of us*. If God is able to forgive us our enormous cache of sin, our forgiveness of the one who has hurt us is small in comparison.

Sometimes in trying to forgive we put an intense but unnecessary burden on ourselves. I thought I could completely forgive right away. But I discovered that forgiveness is not a one-time act. It's a process. While it begins with the *decision* to forgive, it often takes time before the heart fully accepts what the will has set in motion. How long it takes may depend somewhat on the severity of the pain. Forgiveness takes time, and we must give ourselves the grace that our healing requires as we put forgiveness in motion.

Even Joseph, one of the greatest examples of forgiveness in the Bible, allowed the full forgiveness of his brothers to marinate over time. When he first recognized them bowing down to him in Egypt, he did not run out to them with extended arms. After his initial decision to forgive, he tested their hearts. He gave them a chance to reflect on their sin and come to terms with what they had done. And when he finally forgave them, his forgiveness was complete and glorious (Gen. 37:1—45:15).

Fallen Beings

When we have been deeply wronged, something inside yearns for justice. Without a decision to forgive, our desire for justice becomes a longing for retribution or vengeance, subjecting us to the bondage of bitterness and self-righteousness. I eventually realized that for those of us who sincerely choose to forgive, the justice we seek is for the other person *to feel our pain*. For some of us, if we are eventually able to reconcile with our spouses, that day might come. And if it does, one of the things we should discuss as a couple is how to bring the process of forgiveness to a close, mutually forgiving each other for relapses while moving forward to a complete healing.

But for this moment in time, we may have to move forward with forgiveness without expecting *any* form of justice.

True forgiveness takes place when we can release our hurt, acknowledging that our husband is a fallen human being who is incomplete in himself and who is perhaps doing the best he can with the limited resources he has in his emotional, relational, and spiritual arsenal. When we anchor our hearts on the rock of God's mighty love and release our pain into God's compassionate understanding and care, forgiveness becomes part of God's higher purpose and his eternal plan.

The mystery is that when we pierce our own heart by erasing the debt that is owed, when we sacrificially do what seems unnatural instead of exacting revenge, our gift of forgiveness brings freedom and relief to the deep ache of our soul. Instead of holding onto the pain, we open our inner self to the healing ministry of our loving Father, who is the ultimate forgiver. The act of forgiveness is like standing beneath a waterfall and feeling the cool, refreshing water spill over our bodies, washing the pain from our hearts. The rush of freedom, release, and exhilaration is exquisite. As the living water of God's love rolls through us in a stream of forgiveness to our spouse, it cleanses our heart and opens it up to God so he can place more of his image within us.

What at first seems so painful, lightens our step, erases the wrinkles from our brow, and brings joy back into our heart.

> Dear Father, help me forgive. You know the excruciating pain of my heart. You know I don't want to forgive my husband. I want to see him pay for the hurt he has caused me. But, Father, I want to submit myself to your will and your ways. I want to understand your heart of love and become a part of your deeper mysteries. Strengthen my heart to follow your example. You have forgiven me of so much. Let me also find the will to forgive my husband.

LOVE'S PARADOX

*This is love: not that we loved God,
but that he loved us and sent his Son as an
atoning sacrifice for our sins.*

—1 JOHN 4:10

*W*hen my daughter Laura moved into a new apartment, her roommate brought her a stray puppy. It was wild and unmanageable, nipping at her feet, chewing up favorite possessions, crying all night. Friends told her to get rid of him. But Laura loved him. She cuddled with him at night and treated him with a tenderness that soothed his untamed spirit. She gave of herself beyond what she as a young woman had ever done before. Clyde was an unworthy puppy, not special in anyone's eyes but hers. But through her love, he became a wonderful, loving, loyal pet.

As women, being loved by our husbands is of paramount importance. The value we have in our own eyes often depends on whether we feel loved by him—or someone else. Being loved—that is what makes us feel special. That is how we think. That is how we feel.

But the truth is actually just the opposite. The one who is loved is simply the receiver—like Clyde. The one who does the loving reaches down inside her being to draw out something bigger than herself to give away. She becomes more than herself. She becomes special by loving.

When we compare ourselves to God, we can again see the distinction. God so loved us that he sacrificed his Son so we could live—that is love. He, the lover, is far more worthy than we, who are simply the receivers of his deep sacrificial love. God loves us, not because we are so good, but because *he* is so good. It is his *nature* to love us. God is the one who is awesome.

When we struggle with our feelings of worth, when we no longer feel special or beautiful because we are not receiving our husband's love, we need to remember the model given by God himself. The one who loves is the one who is beautiful. We become more beautiful when we learn to love with God's love.

And that is the true test that God asks of us. God desires that we love as he loves—sacrificially from the depth of a heart submitted to him, broken and softened, and open to the wild and passionate flood of God's Holy Spirit. God asks us to do what humans by ourselves cannot do: to love the unworthy, to love the unlovable—even to love the man who wronged us.

For God so loved the world that
he gave his one and only Son.

—John 3:16

THE POWER OF PRAISE

Sing to God, sing praise to his name,
extol him who rides on the clouds—his name is
the LORD—and rejoice before him.

—Psalm 68:4

The stars formed a canopy above us as we breathed in the fragrance of pine and crisp mountain air. In the distance the commanding mountain range that defined the campground was now in shadow, barely visible in the blazing light of our campfire. Strains of a favorite song soared through the branches of the trees, the lilting chorus mounting on the air as the other campers and I proclaimed the awesome wonder of a God who created the splendor of the universe. I truly felt that I was touching the heart of God. It was an exquisite taste of heaven.

For years I called it a mountaintop experience because I thought I had to be in the mountains, in nature, to feel the presence of God surrounding me so richly. It was many years before I learned that I was simply experiencing the first blushes of an amazing truth of God—the power of praise.

God is an awesome God, and when we fully wrap our minds and hearts around that truth, it is difficult to constrain ourselves. Somehow just uttering those words and lifting our voices in praise cuts through the dimensions of two worlds, and a bit of eternity breaks through our earthly habitat.

It is one thing to consider praising God when things are going well, when prayers have been answered, when blessings fill our lives. *But praising God in the midst of our brokenness?* How is that even possible? How can words of praise even form on our lips when our breath is weighted with sighs?

God Inhabits Our Praise

One of the most mysterious and incredible revelations in the Bible is found in an unassuming verse, Psalm 22:3: "Thou art holy, O thou that *inhabitest* the praises of Israel" (KJV). It refers to the Israelites, but it is talking about us as well. It says God inhabits our praises. When we praise God from the heart, he is here in our midst.

"I will extol the LORD at all times," says David in Psalm 34:1–2, "his praise will always be on my lips. My soul will boast in the LORD; let the afflicted hear and rejoice."

God is with us always—in our everyday life, in our pain, in our joys, in our prayerful supplications. But he *inhabits* our praise. When we praise him, we open up our hearts and our lives to him; we invite him in and give him permission to fully bless us and do his deepest work.

When Mary, the mother of Jesus, went to visit her cousin Elizabeth early in Mary's pregnancy, Elizabeth immediately affirmed her as the mother of the Messiah. Mary offered a beautiful song of praise. "My soul magnifies the Lord, and my spirit rejoices in God my Savior" (Luke 1:46–47 RSV). At that moment, as she *magnified* the Lord, the eternal purpose of the plan God had written her name into became exalted and enlarged in her mind. God was magnified in her eyes; she was minimized. The troubling circumstance of being pregnant though unmarried was dwarfed in the light of the magnitude of his eternal purpose for mankind. What she needed was to see the larger plan behind the awkwardness of her situation, and God gave her that vision in the midst of her praise.

When we turn our minds to the wonder of God instead of the bleakness of our circumstances, God becomes magnified.

He becomes larger and our circumstances seem less significant by comparison. His truth and love transform our reality. Our problems fade as we see through the prism of eternity. Praise brings us into the very presence of God and draws him into the circumstances of our lives. What happens next depends on our soul's deepest longings and needs.

During the years of my separation, when I felt myself slipping into depression, I would often insert a praise album into my tape player at home or in the car, and immediately I felt a rush of relief as God lifted my spirit toward him. I could focus on him and push away the clouds of despair.

However, the most exquisite experience with praise came at a time when my husband and I were beginning to reconcile. My emotions continued to pull me in different directions. In an extended praise service, as I worshipped and praised God from the depths of my heart, I felt the Holy Spirit washing through my emotions, churning through the memories, draining the anguish from my soul, cleansing away my pain to replace it with his peace.

Connecting with God

When the people marched around outside the walls of Jericho singing and praising God, the walls fell down (Josh. 6:2–20). God was in their midst as they praised him, and he brought them victory. We may not bring down physical walls with our singing, but praising God can bring down spiritual walls, emotional walls, and the walls that separate people as we focus on our Lord and release our stubborn wills into his care. Praise connects us to God's heart so that we not only experience his presence but hear his voice.

So what happens when an all-seeing, all-knowing, all-powerful God invades our circumstances? What happens when our small world of pain is pierced by eternity? Our lives and our pain are transformed. Peace reigns instead.

Praise is the most intimate way we connect to God. As we acknowledge who he is, as we humble ourselves and magnify him, we draw God into our circumstances. He pushes out our worries and fear, our attitude of unforgiveness, our pain, our selfish desires, our confusion. He brings peace and joy to our troubled spirits. He gives us a fresh revelation of his love. He heals our emotions and deep hurts, and he transforms the inner places of our souls so that within us soars a chorus of praise acknowledging the Alpha and Omega, the First and the Last, our everlasting and faithful God.

We don't know where God is leading us or what the end of this story will look like. But we know who is on this path with us. We know that our everlasting Father is in control and he is the giver of good gifts. When we praise him for who he is, we allow him to release the full measure of the blessings he is storing up for us. We can praise him for his power, love, and mercy, which is all we need because he is our Father, and his desire is to bless us with the riches of heaven.

I will exalt you, my God the King; I will praise your name for ever and ever. Every day I will praise you and extol your name for ever and ever. Great is the Lord and most worthy of praise; his greatness no one can fathom. One generation will commend your works to another; they will tell of your mighty acts. They will speak of the glorious splendor of your majesty, and I will meditate on your wonderful works.

—PSALM 145:1–5

WALKING ON THE WATER

Jesus immediately said to [his disciples]: "Take courage! It is I. Don't be afraid." "Lord, if it's

*you," Peter replied, "tell me to come to you on
the water." "Come," he said. Then Peter got
down out of the boat, walked on the water and
came toward Jesus. But when he saw the wind,
he was afraid and, beginning to sink, cried out,
"Lord, save me!" Immediately Jesus reached out
his hand and caught him.*

—MATTHEW 14:27–31

*H*ow we want a miracle! We look to Jesus walking on the
water, his feet taking great strides above the foaming
waves, his robes blowing in the wind as he approaches. The
powers of this world cannot hold him back. He is the
Overcomer, the Mighty One. He is coming toward us. He is
speaking to us. "It is I," he says.

We meet his gaze and feel drawn into the circle of his love
and strength. We want to join him. We want to walk on the
water too. We want to plow through the storm and trample the
threatening waters and know the safety of being with him. And
with our eyes on Jesus, we step out of the boat.

That's what Peter did. His faith and his desire to be with
Jesus gave him the courage to step onto the waves, and amaz-
ingly he actually did it. He actually walked toward Jesus on the
water. But despite his bravery, when he looked at the waves
surging around him, he became afraid and began to sink.

Even as we exercise great faith, fear rises up in us at times,
and we feel as though we are sinking. We feel overwhelmed.

We don't know how far Peter had to walk to get to Jesus, but
the farther it was, the greater the potential for fear to set in. The
longer our trial lasts, the more we realize how weak we are and
how much we need Jesus. We try to hold on by ourselves, but
we can't. And we don't have to.

Jesus comes to us now, inviting us to join him as he strides
through the tempest and treads on the menacing waves. With
his power, we are able to walk on the water like Peter did, and
if we keep our eyes on Jesus, we will make it through the rising

tides. When our faith grows weak—as it will—and we call out to him, his hand reaches out to us, and through his strength we are able to hold on.

But we can't look down, and we can't look back. We must press on toward the goal and keep our eyes on Jesus. He is the mighty God, and he alone holds us safely above the swirling waters. Christ holds the victory in his hand, and he wants to share it with us.

> Jesus, help me. Hold me up when I get weak. Give me the will to continue when I'd rather stay in the boat. Let me walk with you on the water. Let me experience the victory you are waiting to give me.

Epilogue

> *The poor and needy search for water, but there is none; their tongues are parched with thirst. But I the LORD will answer them; I, the God of Israel, will not forsake them. I will make rivers flow on barren heights, and springs within the valleys. I will turn the desert into pools of water, and the parched ground into springs.*
> —Isaiah 41:17–18

For days the sun had not shone. And for sunny Florida, two weeks of steady rain was unusual.

The sky had intermittently dripped and poured and sprinkled, with an occasional reprieve of an hour or two when the clouds hung dark and heavy. At those times the moisture did not come from the skies but from our own bodies; perspiration hugged our skin in the cool humidity. One day after another, the rain continued.

As I emerged from the front door one afternoon to take the dog around the block, moisture still clung to the blades of St. Augustine grass. The pavement was wet beneath the oak trees. But as I rounded a corner and looked out from the cover of branches above me, blue skies and wispy clouds greeted me. Birds chirruped happily in the trees. A lightness filled my step. My spirit rose. The sun was beginning to shine.

Dear God, how I love happy endings. I love sunshine after a rain and the rainbow after a storm. I hate pain and suffering and anger and bitterness. But sometimes in this world, happy endings seem possible only in the movies. Real life doesn't seem to work out that way.

But, God, in your Word you promise a happy ending. In Psalm 126:5 you promise that those who sow in tears shall reap in joy. Isaiah 61:3 promises to give beauty instead of ashes and the oil of joy in place of mourning. But best of all, Lord, you have promised to give me hope and a future. It's right there in Jeremiah 29:11: "I know the plans I have for you ... plans to prosper you and not to harm you, plans to give you hope and a future."

I will cling to these promises, Lord, and believe that as the following days unfold, you will be walking beside me in the storm, revealing new truths and fulfilling all my needs. I put my future in your hands and trust that you will turn the desert of my life into pools of water and the parched ground into springs. In Jesus' powerful name I pray, Amen.

He holds victory in store for the upright.
—PROVERBS 2:7

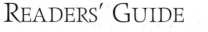 Readers' Guide

Life is difficult. While that seems a no-brainer, we all secretly hope we will win the life-is-easy lottery and have no or few difficult moments in our lives.

This is especially true when it comes to marriage. We agree intellectually that it can be hard to blend two independent, often slightly (or more than slightly) dysfunctional lives into a healthy, whole one. However, that intellectual assent is about as sturdy as a house of cards in a windstorm. What we *really* believe is that our love is strong enough to carry us through any hardship, and we will live happily ever after, safe and snug in our ardor for each other. Any and all troubles will be minor. We will respect and cherish each other without fail, and our children will rise up and call us blessed.

Well, of course that's the way it is supposed to be.

But life *is* difficult, and people are flawed. Attitudes sour. People misbehave. Relationships can and do go wrong.

For whatever reason you now find yourself in the wreckage of a failed marriage. Your heart has been broken—and so have your illusions, your hopes, and your dreams. You may struggle with a kaleidoscope of shifting emotions—confusion, betrayal, fear, bitterness, denial, low self-esteem, failure, and shame. These emotions sap you of strength, leaving you feeling helpless to cope with your spouse's rejection.

This book is not designed to simply make you feel better. Soothing words will not change your marital situation. A Scripture verse will not magically bring back your spouse and radically change him for the better. But as you read *Broken Heart on Hold* and prayerfully and honestly journal your thoughts and responses to the study guide questions, you may find yourself gaining new perspectives, developing new strengths, and experiencing more emotional and spiritual peace.

You may want to keep this as a time just for you and your loving heavenly Father. He will not judge or criticize you as you share your responses with him. He is the ultimate lover, the adoring bridegroom, the God who loves unconditionally. Let him love you as you spend time reading and meditating on each chapter.

Or you may prefer to work through *Broken Heart on Hold* with a spiritually mature friend or a small group. The support of faithful friends and the insight they may offer can add to the benefit you get from this book. Either way, our prayer is that this book and this study guide will help you in the healing process.

Part 1
HOLDING TOGETHER A BREAKING HEART

1. Sometimes we shut others out when we're hurting. Are you doing that with God? He is your healer, counselor, and comforter. Look to his Word and find some promises of love and healing you can cling to. Spend time in a Psalm or other favorite passages. Write it in your journal or memorize and repeat it daily. You might begin with 1 Peter 5:10.

2. The Bible tells us not to sin in the midst of our anger: "Be angry but do not sin" (Eph. 4:26 RSV). How are you tempted to sin—to harm yourself or others—in expressing your anger? Does it seem unfair to have to exercise self-restraint when you've been so deeply injured? Journal your thoughts and feelings, and ask God to calm the raging emotions within.

3. Rejection one day, roses the next. Are you getting mixed messages from your spouse? What resources (such as prayer, friends, or the Bible) are you comfortable seeking to help sort through these issues? How can you make these regular strengths in your life?

4. Are you keeping a journal? If so, write down the "legs of the stool" that are distracting you now from your focus on God. Ask him to help you let go of the distractions, and entrust him with them. Then take some time to focus on the lover of your soul. Meditate on this verse: "Be still, and know that I am God" (Ps. 46:10).

5. Some people love the dizzying swoop and ascent and plunge of the roller coaster. Others hate it. Your roller-coaster emotions may seem terrifying and as if they'd last forever. But God can belt you in safely and take you through this turbulent period to a calmer, more emotionally stable time. What counsel do you find in God's Word to help you with your emotions? If you are unsure, who can help you find such counsel?

6. Do you think of your friends as God's love gifts? Take some time to journal what they mean to you and how each can minister to you, whether through a cup of coffee and a long chat, a brisk walk, or a

time together in God's Word. Also consider how you can support them. Thank God for the friends in your life.

7. What advice would you give a friend whose health was at risk due to severe stress? How can you apply that same advice to your life as you care for yourself?

8. "For I am convinced that neither death nor life, neither angels nor demons, neither the present nor the future, nor any powers, neither height nor depth, nor anything else in all creation, will be able to separate us from the love of God that is in Christ Jesus our Lord" (Rom. 8:38–39). Do you really believe God is all-powerful and loving? You have an opportunity now to discover his faithfulness as you rest in him.

9. "Forgive us our sins, for we also forgive everyone who sins against us" (Luke 11:4). Forgiving isn't excusing bad behavior, but bad behavior doesn't excuse a lack of forgiveness, either. A godly attitude may take time and lots of prayer, but it's necessary for our spiritual and emotional health. What steps can you take toward forgiveness today?

10. Your pain and panic are temporary. God's love is enduring. When emotions threaten to overwhelm you, remind yourself of his deep, abiding love for you. What ways are most effective personally for you to focus on Jesus?

11. Now that you've presented the Lord with your "gift" of your worries and fears, what productive ways can you find to use your time to improve your home and family life?

12. Are you ready to go deeper in the Lord, listening to his voice and obeying his nudges? What stands in the way of your doing so? What small steps can you take to draw near to him?

13. "My people have committed two sins: they have forsaken me, the spring of living water, and have dug their own cisterns, broken cisterns that cannot hold water" (Jer. 2:13). Meditate on this verse and journal your thoughts on it. In what ways have you dug broken cisterns—wells—to have your needs met?

Part 2
A SAFE PLACE FOR YOUR HEART

1. "Can a mother forget the baby at her breast and have no compassion on the child she has borne? Though she may forget, I will not forget you! See, I have engraved you on the palms of my hands" (Isa. 49:15–16). Take a few moments now to lean into God's unchanging love and feel his strength and constant, tender care for you.

2. "You are my hiding place; you will protect me from trouble and surround me with songs of deliverance" (Ps. 32:7).
    "You are my fortress, my refuge in times of trouble" (Ps. 59:16).
    Write these verses on a note card and post them on your bathroom mirror, in your kitchen, on your nightstand—wherever they will help remind you of God's protective care. When you look at them, take a moment to thank and praise him, even if it's for just one thing.

3. What verse or verses did you pick to help you battle fear and worry? Share them with a friend who can help encourage you to keep your focus on God's promises.

4. Waiting is hard, especially since we can't see the future. But the time goes by faster if we occupy our minds and hands productively. What are some ways you can use this time well as you wait to see God at work in your relationship?

5. It may seem as though the locusts have ravaged all the fruit of your life, but if you look closely, you'll find precious fruit intact. Take some time to reflect on and journal some of the lasting fruit in your life.

6. Nutritionists tell us our bodies are dehydrated well before we actually feel thirsty. Are you spiritually dehydrated? Even if you don't feel you are, you need to take time to replenish your spirit. How can you do that today?

7. The author made an extra effort to focus on Jesus at a time when she knew she was emotionally vulnerable. However, this doesn't mean she denied or refused to work through her emotions. For everything

there is a season—how do you decide when to deal with emotions and when to look beyond them?

8. How would you rate your buoyancy level? Are you afloat or sinking into depression? If despite your best efforts to look to Jesus to lift your spirits you can't find peace, seek medical help or a professional counselor. Don't consider it a lapse of faith—God uses doctors to help heal us.

9. Does your life feel like a giant, mystifying puzzle—with one or more pieces missing? What can you do today to trust all the pieces to God?

10. Do you agree that it's the form of your marriage that needs to change? What shape would your marriage take if you could change it by your own actions?

11. Put yourself in Penny's shoes. How would you have handled Nick's infidelity? How are you handling your own sense of having been wronged in your marriage? While your circumstances are different, how can you apply the same godly principles of love, forgiveness, and mercy?

Part 3
SEARCHING YOUR HEART

1. How are you tempted to escape this difficult time of life? Ask God to help you be willing to yield yourself to his greater purpose, to make something good from your suffering.

2. Are you just going through the motions spiritually—or are you actively seeking to go deeper with the Lord? What does it mean to you to "go deeper"?

3. Are you able to see what part you played in the crumbling of your marriage? Ask God for the courage and clarity to see and acknowledge your own sins. Consider writing a letter to your spouse to ask forgiveness.

4. If God is pulling weeds in your life, he may ask you to give him a hand. Trust that even as he weeds and prunes, he's also planting and

nurturing fruit in your life as you let him. Pray that he will also do that in your husband's life.

5. To help you trust God as you travel the detour life has taken you on, consider the "divine detours" he's led you on in the past. What blessings did you receive from these unexpected detours?

6. What stage in the grief process are you experiencing most? Do you need help getting unstuck from the depression, grief, or anger stages? If so, ask God to help lead you through the stages to acceptance and peace. Let him be your guide.

7. Do you daydream of ways to get even with your spouse? It may feel satisfying at the moment, but retribution won't heal your pain or resolve your differences. Use your daydreaming time to consider ways to bless and forgive your spouse instead.

8. "You intended to harm me, but God intended it for good to accomplish what is now being done" (Gen. 50:20). Ask God to reveal to you some of what he's doing to redeem your painful situation. Is he strengthening your character, making you more sensitive to others, driving you to rely more deeply on him? Thank him for the work he's doing and will continue to do in you.

9. The author stated, "You may be the only priest God has available to bring your husband back to him." Are you willing to be God's priest to the one who has hurt you so deeply? If anything hinders you from praying for his salvation or relationship with God, confess it now to the Lord, then lift a heartfelt prayer to God for your spouse to return to him.

10. Prayer is vital during the challenging times we face. How can you make prayer a more integral way of life?

11. Can you count this difficult trial you're in as "pure joy" as it says in James 1:2? Maybe not yet. Can you at least agree with God to be fashioned into "pure gold" as your faith is hammered out in the fire of adversity? "When he has tested me, I will come forth as gold" (Job 23:10).

12. Do you ever feel like King Saul—impatient to hurry God along and get things done in your own timing? Pray that you'll be sensitive and obedient to his timing, so you don't miss his blessings.

13. Are you willing to follow God as Abraham did—one day, one step at a time? Are you willing to be willing?

Part 4
HEART CONNECTIONS:
WALKING THROUGH THE SHARDS

1. Do you feel beautiful and loved? Take a moment to soak in the knowledge that God finds you beautiful and loves you just as you are.

2. Write your own poem, song, or reflection on where you are with God and your spouse right now. Are you able to see this time as a sweet dependence on God?

3. "The Sovereign LORD is my strength! He will make me as surefooted as a deer and bring me safely over the mountains" (Hab. 3:19 NLT). Picture yourself as a mountain climber. Where are you now in your journey? Climbing a sheer wall? In a green and pleasant valley? What Scriptures confirm God's power to keep you safe as you encounter difficult life passages?

4. How well-equipped a soldier are you in God's army? Take an inventory of your armor by meditating on Ephesians 6:10–18. Ask God to show you where your battle skills need some work.

5. "He who guards his lips guards his life, but he who speaks rashly will come to ruin" (Prov. 13:3). Have you found a safe, wise friend or family member to talk to? Write out the qualities that would make for a good, appropriate listener—and don't settle for less.

6. What words of encouragement or discouragement have you been getting from friends and acquaintances? Journal them and ask God for

discernment in seeing what to sift out and what to keep. Pray for friends whose words will help you grow in spiritual strength and wisdom.

7. Children often don't know how to express their pain and confusion at their parents' separation. They may feel responsible. They may blame one parent for all the problems that caused the marriage's collapse. Just as you need emotional and spiritual support, so do they. What church and other resources are available to help them through this difficult time? Which are you comfortable utilizing?

8. The author pointed out that "it is when we are the weakest that Satan tries to attack." What steps can you take to fortify your heart against temptation?

9. "The LORD has already told you what is good, and this is what he requires: to do what is right, to love mercy, and to walk humbly with your God" (Mic. 6:8 NLT). What does it look like to walk humbly with God in the midst of your broken marriage? What does it mean to you that you and your spouse are saved by grace?

10. "If we have nothing, he can be everything," the author reminds us. What is the "everything" you need God to be for you today? Thank him that he is—and gives—even more than you can imagine asking.

11. Ask God to reveal to you how to engage in spiritual warfare for your husband and yourself. Go back to Ephesians 6:10–18 and strap on the armor of God. "Use every piece of God's armor to resist the enemy in the time of evil, so that after the battle you will still be standing firm" (Eph. 6:13 NLT).

12. "Greater is he that is in you, than he that is in the world" (1 John 4:4 KJV). Do you truly believe that? What are some practical and healing things you can pray for your husband, regardless of what the future holds? How can it help you to lift your husband's spiritual well-being before the Lord?

13. Small changes can have a ripple effect for good. What steps can you take to change your attitudes and behavior for the better? "Let God transform you into a new person by changing the way you think. Then

you will know what God wants you to do, and you will know how good and pleasing and perfect his will really is" (Rom. 12:2 NLT).

14. According to the author, "If you have an emotionally or spiritually scarred spouse, you may have to be like the horse whisperer. The only thing you may be able to do right now is to sit and wait." Sometimes God speaks truth through our culture and arts. Rent or borrow a copy of *The Horse Whisperer* and watch it prayerfully, asking God how you can learn patience and kindness from the movie's example.

15. Can you let go of your marriage and your spouse and cling to God instead? In what areas of your life do you find it difficult to give up control?

16. Do you need emotional or physical distance from your spouse? Use the time apart to draw even closer to the Lord—and let him be the husband of your soul.

17. Small and large distractions can keep us from seeking God's presence, but that's exactly where we need to be if we're going to find the strength to tackle each day's struggles. What keeps you from abiding in Christ daily? Write down some practical ways you can grow closer to him.

18. What are your thoughts about Kimberly and Aaron's story? What kind of growth did it take on both their parts before they were able to start afresh? What would it take for you and your husband to start over?

Part 5
A RESTORED HEART

1. The author said, "When we're in a crisis, no matter where we run, we'll still be in the crisis—whether we hold onto the ball, drop it, or fall down and let life's burdens topple on top of us. So we might as well 'hold on to the ball and get the touchdown.'" In what ways does this philosophy seem realistic or unrealistic to you? What can you do to stand firm in the midst of life's crises—and make the winning touchdown?

2. Do you feel the arrows of self-pity, resentment, bitterness, or lack of faith assaulting you? Don't wait until they've scorched you—wear the armor of God daily so they never find a vulnerable place to penetrate. Write down some strategies for defending yourself against Satan's attacks.

3. What stands in the way of forgiving your husband? Repeated grievances against you? His lack of remorse? Fear that he might hurt you worse if you were to forgive him? A secret enjoyment of being the wronged party? Whatever stands in your way, it also hinders you from true spiritual and emotional freedom. Ask God to reveal where you need to forgive and to give you the strength to do it.

4. The author points out that "the one who loves is the one who is beautiful. We become more beautiful when we learn to love with God's love." How can you begin to appropriate the truth in these words and live by them? Perhaps you can begin today by loving your spouse enough to pray in earnest that God will bless and lead him into all righteousness.

5. What does it mean to you that God inhabits our praises? Do you have a deeper sense of his presence when you praise him? Do you believe there's power in praise? Ask him to reveal through his Word the power of praise, then spend time worshipping him.

6. Does it seem strange to think you could "walk on water" in the midst of pain and rejection? As you deal with the turbulent storm of your broken relationship, envision yourself holding on to the hand that Jesus is reaching out to you. Find your "walking on water" verse to help give you hope in times when you feel you're going to sink. Here's one to consider: "'For I know the plans I have for you,' declares the LORD, 'plans to prosper you and not to harm you, plans to give you hope and a future'" (Jer. 29:11).

RECOMMENDED RESOURCES

PROGRAMS AND MARRIAGE SEMINARS

Retrouvaille—Reconciling your marriage, 800-470-2230; www.retrouvaille.org
Reconciling God's Way—Reconciling your marriage, 800-205-6808;
www.reconcilinggodsway.org
Crown Financial Ministries—Financial problems, 800-722-1976;
www.crown.org

INTERNET SITES

www.marriagebuilders.com
www.marriagesavers.org
www.family.org (search for topic)

BOOKS

ABUSE
Allender, Dan B. *The Wounded Heart*. Colorado Springs: NavPress, 1990.
Hegstrom, Paul. *Angry Men and the Women Who Love Them*. Kansas City: Beacon
    Hill, 2004.
Stewart, Donald. *Refuge*. Birmingham, AL: New Hope, 2004.

ADDICTION
Al-Anon Family Group Headquarters, Inc. *The Dilemma of the Alcoholic Mar-
    riage*. Virginia Beach, VA: Al-Anon Family Group Headquarters, Inc.,
    1981.
Nakken, Craig. *The Addictive Personality*. Center City, MN: Hazelden, 1996.

ANGER
Carlson, Dwight L. *Overcoming Hurts and Anger*. Eugene, OR: Harvest House,
    2000.
Carter, Les, and Frank Minirth. *Anger Workbook*. Nashville: Thomas Nelson, 1992.

ATTENTION DEFICIT DISORDER (ADD)
Amen, Daniel G. *Healing ADD*. New York: Berkley, 2002.
Hartmann, Thom. *Attention Deficit Disorder, A Different Perception*. Nevada City,
    CA: Underwood Books, 1997.

CONTROL ISSUES
Carter, Les. *Imperative People.* Nashville: Thomas Nelson, 1992.
Cloud, Henry, and John Townsend. *Boundaries in Marriage.* Grand Rapids, MI: Zondervan, 2002.
Hunter, Becky. *Being Good to Your Husband on Purpose.* Lake Mary, FL: Strang Communications, 2001.

DIVORCE RECOVERY HELP
Petherbridge, Laura. *When Your Marriage Dies.* Colorado Springs: Life Journey, Cook Communications, 2005.

FORGIVENESS
Carlson, Dwight. *Overcoming Hurts and Anger.* Eugene, OR: Harvest House, 2000.
Kendall, R. T. *Total Forgiveness.* Lake Mary, FL: Strang Communications, 2002.

INFIDELITY
Anderson, Nancy C. *Avoiding the Greener Grass Syndrome.* Grand Rapids, MI: Kregel, 2004.
Dobson, James. *Love Must Be Tough.* Sisters, OR: Multnomah, 2004.
Rosenau, Douglas. *Slaying the Marriage Dragons.* Colorado Springs: Victor Books, Cook Communications, 1991.
Shriver, Gary, and Mona Shriver. *Unfaithful.* Colorado Springs: Life Journey, Cook Communications, 2005.

MEN/WOMEN ISSUES
Gray, John. *Men Are From Mars, Women Are From Venus.* New York: Harper-Collins, 2004.

MID-LIFE CRISIS
Conway, Jim. *Men in Mid-Life Crisis.* Colorado Springs: Victor Books, Cook Communications, 1997.
Morley, Patrick. *Second Wind for the Second Half.* Grand Rapids, MI: Zondervan, 1999.

PAINFUL RELATIONSHIPS
Gray, John. *What You Feel You Can Heal.* Broomall, PA: Heart, 1994.

PORNOGRAPHY
Arterburn, Stephen, and Fred Stoeker. *Every Man's Battle.* Colorado Springs: Waterbrook, 2000.
Arterburn, Stephen, and Fred and Brenda Stoeker. *Every Heart Restored.* Colorado Springs: Waterbrook, 2004.

SEPARATION
Clinton, Tim. *Before a Bad Goodbye.* Nashville: Word, 1999.

SEXUAL PROBLEMS
LaHaye, Tim, and Beverly LaHaye. *The Act of Marriage.* Grand Rapids, MI: Zondervan, 1998.

SPIRITUAL GROWTH
Curtis, Brent, and John Eldredge. *Sacred Romance.* Nashville: Thomas Nelson, 1997.
Lewis, C. S. *Mere Christianity.* San Francisco: HarperSanFrancisco, 2001.
Marshall, Catherine. *Beyond Ourselves.* New York: Avon Books, 1994.

SPIRITUAL WARFARE
Barnhouse, Donald Grey. *The Invisible War.* Grand Rapids, MI: Zondervan, 1980.
Montgomery, Leslie. *Engaging the Enemy.* Colorado Springs: Life Journey, Cook Communications, 2006.
Prince, Derek. *Spiritual Warfare.* New Kensington, PA: Whitaker House, 2001.

STRENGTHENING MARRIAGE
Harley, Jr., Willard F. *His Needs, Her Needs.* Grand Rapids, MI: Fleming H. Revell, 2001.
Omartian, Stormie. *The Power of a Praying Wife.* Eugene, OR: Harvest House, 1997.

SCRIPTURE FOR ENCOURAGEMENT AND HOPE

The author's Web site, www.brokenheartonhold.com, provides full-color pages of Scripture verses in large format available for download. These can be used as points of focus throughout your house to give you extra encouragement. The Web site also features author information and valuable links.

TOPICAL INDEX

A

Abandonment, 91–92, 159
Abram, 105
Abuse, 95, 142
Acceptance in the grief process, 89
Adultery, 91, 126
Advice, 91, 99, 118, 121, 146
Affair, 126–27
Alone, 14, 81, 120, 154, 157
Amanda's story, 39–43, 120
Anger
  control of, 32–33
  controlled expression, 92–94
  expressing of, 18
  in the grief process, 89
  releasing, 18
  unseen battle, 130–32
Answer, 11, 23, 99
Anxiety, 24, 37, 54, 87, 105
Armor of God, 117, 157–62
Attitude, 31, 39, 69, 135, 137

B

Back burner, 37–38
Beach ball, 64–65
Beauty and God's love, 112–13
Beginning of our madness, 19–22
Betrayal, 33, 35, 175
Beyond broken dreams, 14–15
Bible
  anger without sin, 32–33

God inhabits our praises, 168
God's relationship with people, 53
  as playbook, 60, 62
  temptation, 127
Bitterness of anger, 32
Books, 66, 187–89

C

Change, 70, 109, 129, 142–45
Chicken soup, 61–62
Children
  impact of bitterness, 32
  impact of godless chatter, 119
  impact of marriage separation, 123–25
  independence, 58
  punishment, 116
  reaction to parent's pain, 17–18
Christian, 16, 27, 28, 38, 132
Church, 27, 75
Coffee break with God, 36–37
Comfort, 12, 19, 47
Commitment of marriage, 16, 143
Communication, 76, 109, 137, 139
Conflict, 107
Confusion, 23–24, 34–35, 123
Control
  anger and, 32
  lion-tamer, 23
  of mindset, 33
  of runaway emotions, 34–35
  trusting God, 55, 129, 170

Conviction, 81, 83, 89, 93–94, 99
Coping mechanism, 85
Counseling, 27, 89, 118–19, 127, 145
Crying, 11, 32, 89, 94, 100

D

Dating, 126, 147
David's suffering, 94–95
Dead end, 67, 87
Death of beautiful things, 141–42
Deception of Satan, 132, 160
Decision, 38, 53, 56, 90, 163–64
Deeper in the Christian life, 16, 66, 80–82, 96
Denial in the grief process, 18, 89, 144
Dependence, 62, 101, 113, 159
Depression
  emotional control, 34
  in the grief process, 18, 89
  medications for treatment, 30
  relief from, 57, 65, 90
Despair, 18, 89, 144, 159, 169
Detours, 86–87
Devil, 132. See also Satan
Direction, change of, 142–45
Discipline, 75, 87, 90
Discouragement, 49, 59, 90, 120–22, 160–61
Distance, 54, 144–45
Divorce, 38, 39–43, 68–69
Doormat, 136

Duncan, Barry, 69, 137

E

Eating to stay healthy, 30
Emotions, 24–25, 29, 34–35, 175
Encouragement, 120–22
Enemy, 87, 99, 132–35, 163
Epilogue, 172–74
Eternity, 154–55
Exercise, 18, 28–29, 30

F

Facing a four-legged stool, 22–24
Faith
  author and perfecter of, 66, 85
  given by God, 82, 115–16, 130
  salvation by grace, 128
  shield of, 160, 161
  through trials, 100, 101
Family, 59, 115
Fasting, 63, 108
Fear, 30–31, 54–55, 171–72
Feelings
  changing of, 23
  grief, 89
  healing, 25
  recording in a journal, 18
  Satan's deceptions, 132
  worthlessness, 166
Fighting, 36, 102, 116, 117
Financial problems, 39–40
Flowers for Mother's Day, 19–20
Focus
  during fear, 31
  four-legged stool, 23–24
  on God, 35, 67, 94, 100, 169
  keeping your focus, 62–64

Satan's temptations, 161
  spiritual muscles, 28–29, 101–02
Forgiveness
  from children, 124
  healing and, 129
  importance of, 163–65
  from sin, 53, 83–84, 125, 132, 163–65
  of yourself, 89, 124
Four-legged stool, 22–24
Friends, 26–27, 119–22
Future
  hidden treasure, 58–59
  relationships, 118
  security, 142
  trusting God, 54–55, 78–80, 87, 89, 142, 173

G

Gifford, Kathie Lee, 162–63
Giving up, 100
Gold, 100–2
Gossip, 119
Grace, 33, 82, 124, 128, 164
Gray, John, 25
Grief
  depression and, 65
  process, 18, 89
  sitting in grief, 42, 92
Guilt
  of anger, 18
  in the grief process, 89

H

Harley, Willard, 126
Healing, 18, 51, 56–57, 92–94, 138–39
Health issues during stress, 29–30
Heart palpitations, 30
His Needs, Her Needs, 126
Holding on, 114–16
Hope, 15, 31, 89, 119, 140

Hopeless, 51, 63, 161
The Horse Whisperer, 138
Humility, 81, 83, 94–95, 128–29
Hunger, 61–62
Husband, 41, 48–49, 133–34

I

Impatience, 104
Infidelity, 70–76, 91, 128
Insecurity, 25, 81

J

Job's suffering, 42, 88, 90, 92, 120
Joseph, 95, 164
Journal, 18, 24, 84, 89, 92
Justice, 164

L

Layers, 22, 107, 146
Let's take a walk, 11–12
Letters, 20–21, 25, 83–84
Letting go, 54–55
Listening
  to children, 37, 38, 124–25
  by friends, 27, 119, 122
  to God, 18, 57, 69, 70, 81, 137, 146, 159
Living stones, 98–100
Locusts, 58–59
Loneliness, 107
Love, 47–49, 165–67
Lying, 132, 161

M

Madness, beginning of, 19–22
Marriage, 69, 85, 126, 141
Memories, 28, 146, 163
Migrating birds, 78–80
Military deployment, 20
Mind
  emotions and, 34–35

focusing, 23–24
functions, 116
mindset, 32–33, 35, 39,
    67
renewal, 82, 127, 135
Moses, 87, 95
Mystery, 162–65

N
New marriage, 68–70, 142

O
Obedience, 63, 88, 103–5
*Overcoming Relationship
    Impasses*, 70, 137

P
Pain, 14–15, 90
Pastors, 23, 27, 73–74
Patience, 28, 70, 85,
    104–5, 146
Peace, 33, 34, 84, 169
Perseverance, 84, 101, 159
Power, 28, 115, 124,
    167–68
Praise, 50–51, 167–70
Prayer, 99, 124–25,
    131–35
Prostitution, 70–76
Purpose, 49, 55, 87, 102,
    103
Puzzle, 65–67

Q
Quietness of your heart,
    145–47

R
Reconciliation, 98, 108–9,
    164
Regret, 25, 56, 146
Rejection, 18–19, 126,
    175
Repentance, 84, 98, 99,
    138
Resolution, 56, 107, 113
Resources, 187–89
Respect, 150, 175
Retribution, 33, 90,
    92–94, 164

Ripped apart, 17–19
Road map, 105–10
Rock, Joseph, 69, 137
Roller-coaster emotions,
    24–25
Runaway emotions, 34–35
Running away, 85

S
Sacrifice, 53, 58, 82,
    96–98, 165–66
Safety, 46–47, 119, 172
Sarcasm, 85, 93, 110
Satan, 126–27, 131–35,
    160–61. *See also* Devil
Saul, 94, 103–4
Security, 31, 63, 81,
    123–24, 142
Seeing the end from the
    beginning, 59–61
Self-pity, 85, 134, 161
Self-righteousness, 76,
    128–29, 164
Self-worth, 48, 166
Separation, 119, 126, 144
Shadows, 140
Silver and gold, 100–2
Sin
    anger and, 18, 33, 93
    deceitfulness of, 102
    forgiveness of, 53,
        83–84, 125, 132,
        163–65
    nature of, 33, 48, 49,
        85
    temptations, 126–27
Spiritual awareness, 16
Spiritual muscle, 28–29,
    63–64, 101–2
Spiritual renewal, 56–57,
    82, 127, 137, 144
Spiritual warfare, 99,
    131–35
Standing firm, 157–59
Strength, 19, 56–57,
    114–15, 128–29
Stronghold, 116–17,
    131–32, 134–35, 160
Suffering, 18–19, 78–80,
    88, 90, 94–96

Surrender, 15, 81, 90, 95,
    117

T
Talking, 28, 32, 66, 89
Temper, 36, 68, 148, 151
Temptation, 125–27, 161
Thoughts, 24, 25, 32–33,
    34, 67
Time, 36, 56–57
Time apart, 144–45
Transition, 18, 144
Trials, 96, 100–2, 171
Trust, 47, 54–56, 65–67,
    118–20, 138–39
Truth, 35, 52–53, 137,
    157–58

U
Undertow, 155–57

V
Value, personal, 49
Van Gogh, Vincent, 58–59

W
Waiting, 38, 56–57, 104,
    138–39
Walking on the water,
    170–72
Walls, spiritual, 169
Water into wine, 103–5
Weakness, 53, 128–29,
    159
Weapons, 116–17
Web sites, 12, 187
Weeds, 84–86
*What You Feel, You Can
    Heal*, 25
When it doesn't make
    sense, 15–16
Wisdom, 94, 118, 124,
    157
Withdrawal, 50–51
Worry, 37, 54–55
Worship, 82, 98